THE GAMEDEV BUDGETING HANDBOOK

How to finish your game in time and on budget!

Michael Futter

bithell

Bithell Games | London, UK

Contact@gamedevbizbook.com

Published in the United Kingdom

ISBN: 978-0-9993290-7-8

Although we work to ensure that this book is up-to-date, change (especially in the video game industry) is almost guaranteed. Especially with regard to accounting and legal matters, regulations change frequently. Be sure to consult your accountant and attorney for the most current guidance. Should you find anything that may be in need of updating, clarification, or correction, please email Contact@BithellGames.com or use the mailing address above.

THANKS

Thanks to Mike Bithell, Alexander Sliwinski, and my family.
And, of course, my deepest thanks to everyone that
purchased *The GameDev Business Handbook* and inspired
us to dive deeper with this companion book.

ACKNOWLEDGEMENTS

Ryan Black, McMillan LLP
Robert Brown, Stride PR
Ashly Burch
Steve Gee, Adult Swim Games
Cheryl Gehbauer, Harmonix
Daniel Goldberg, Paradox Interactive
Hilary Henley, McMillan LLP
Nick Johnson, Affect Group
Shams Jorjani, Paradox Interactive
Steven Manship, Ninja Theory
Jayson Napolitano, Scarlet Moon Productions
Derek Neurer, Harmonix
Dale North
Tom Ohle, Evolve PR
Andrew Parsons, Devolver Digital
Rhianna Pratchett
Thomas Puha, Remedy Entertainment
Sudarshan Ranganathan, Ixie Gaming
Michel Ranger, McMillan LLP
Mike Reid, McMillan LLP
Ella Romanos, Ella Romanos LTD
Niko Stark, Remedy Entertainment
Tuukka Taipalvesi, Remedy Entertainment
Stephanie Thoensen, Psyonix
Zoi Vitsentzou, MoGi Group
Dan Walsh, Harmonix
Walt Williams
Austin Wintory

Written by Michael Futter

Publishers Mike Bithell and Alexander Sliwinski
Editor JC Fletcher
Art Chris Furniss
Layout Hugo Tarring

DIGITAL SUPPLEMENTS

As part of our work on *The GameDev Budgeting Handbook*, we
realized that our budgeting lesson needed to be interactive. Static
samples and templates don't do enough to help the concepts sink in.

Instead, we decided to create living supplements that can grow and
change as the industry evolves. You can access the budget samples,
budget templates, and digital appendices at GameDevBizBook.com.

CONTENTS

Introduction   08

01 How do I get started with budgeting?   10

02 How much is my project going to cost each month?   22

03 What does it really cost to hire an employee?   40

04 What will a publisher pay for?   62

05 How do I obtain and pay for music in my game?   74

06 What should I expect when hiring someone to write my game's story?   100

07 How much does voice acting and performance capture cost?   112

08 What's the best way to work with PR?   126

09 How do I budget for all the software I need to make my game?   142

10 Why do I need attorneys and accountants?   150

Epilogue – Advice from the industry   158

Appendix   172

INTRODUCTION—
GETTING STARTED

Firstly, thank you so much for purchasing *The GameDev Budgeting Handbook*. This is intended as a companion to our first book, *The GameDev Business Handbook*.

While you can most certainly use this workbook by itself, we believe you'll get the most out of it alongside *The GameDev Business Handbook.* You can purchase the hardcover directly from Bithell Games (www.gamedevbizbook.com) or on Amazon. The Kindle version is also available through Amazon. There may be other options by the time you're reading this, so head on over to www. gamedevbizbook.com for the latest details.

Anyway, as we wrapped up work on *The GameDev Business Handbook,* we looked at the breadth of topics we covered. Being self-critical (and taking feedback from readers), we realized that the front of the book is filled with heavy information.

We couldn't quite puzzle out a way to ease readers in, because the meaty financial information is so critical to everything discussed later in the book. So we made the call to keep things top-level, and help as many people as possible understand the breadth of business in the video game industry. *The GameDev Business Handbook* is designed to create foundational understanding and inspire inquiry.

We recognize that some readers might come in unable to ask questions, because they don't know what they don't know. *The GameDev Business Handbook* is designed to help aspiring independent developers and those already in the thick of it craft the questions crucial to operating a business.

The GameDev Budgeting Handbook can either be viewed as the next step or a side step. Here, we're going to take a deeper look at

budgeting and finance. If you're picking this up after *The GameDev Business Handbook*, you know what a budget looks like. We've given you the tools for creating your own with our digital supplements (available at gamedevbizbook.com/digital-supplements).

Now it's time to focus on some of the trickier line items, define additional terms, and dissect the process of budgeting even further. If you're coming to the *The GameDev Budgeting Handbook* first because you specifically want to better understand the cost of various aspects that make up a video game, that's cool too. This book is an explainer, breaking down a game budget and the costs behind various elements. We consulted directly with the talented people working in the industry right now in order to get the most current and detailed information available.

Thanks for taking this trip with us. We're so grateful for your support.

CHAPTER
ONE

HOW DO I GET STARTED WITH BUDGETING?

The video game industry is full of good ideas. If you're an aspiring or active developer, your mind is likely full of brilliant concepts before you even have your morning beverage of choice.

Good ideas get the ball rolling. But if you're serious about turning "wouldn't it be cool if…" into "let's do this" (and selling the results to people,) you're going to need a budget. Your budget is your financial road map. It shows your destination and gives you an idea of how you'll get from where you are to where you'll be when your game is completed and available for sale.

While we can't draw you a personalized map through your project, we can give you the tools. We can help you sketch your own path through the maze, using reference points from those who have been where you are.

The budget will give you starting and ending points. It may even help you identify landmarks at key points on your journey. What it won't give you is turn-by-turn directions. The sat-nav of hand-holding artificial intelligence who can fully assist with game budgeting is still (tragically) decades away.

A budget will (hopefully) tell you that you'll spend less than the cash you'll have during development. In order to figure out if you'll have the money you need when bills come due, you need to project for revenue and expenses on a month-by-month basis. For that, you need to wrangle your **cash flow.**[1]

It doesn't do you any good to anticipate enough money in the bank at the end of the project if you're going to fall short on paying your staff, rent, or software licensing. Thankfully, we've got you covered with budget templates and samples that include a cash flow calculator.

Those tools are available to you in interactive format. You can view them at gamedevbizbook.com/digital-supplements. The cornerstones of this toolbox are the budget samples and templates.

Within that spreadsheet you'll find three samples that cover the following scenarios:

- Your first project without revenue from sales of other games or external funding
- Your first project with external funding from a publisher
- A project with significant external funding from a publisher

In this chapter, we've also included full explanations of how those budgets were compiled and what each line item represents. The spreadsheet includes three templates that allow you to create your own budgets in each of these categories. A full explanation of how to use and customize those can be found in the appendix.

UNDERSTANDING THE BUDGET SAMPLES AND TEMPLATES

Putting together a budget can be daunting if you've never done it before. Before you dive in and start tinkering with your own budget, take some time to check out the samples with embedded comments. This will give you a strong idea of how these look when complete.

---

[1] **Cash flow** - The total amount of money entering and exiting a business over a period of time.

Rather than send you off with just the numbers, we've created the following narratives to set the stage and provide some context.

This way, you'll have a sense of the decision-making that went into each sample. Hopefully, you'll be able to find similarities to your own situation.

Note that these templates contain a variety of formulas. Some knowledge of spreadsheets is helpful, but we've noted how the formulas work, so you can add columns and rows to better represent your own situation.

The columns represent development time, and you may need to add or remove columns. As you do this and add **dev-hours**[2] to the cells, you'll see the direct impact on your project budget.

Ultimately, this leads to the **dev-month**[3] calculation (we'll get into dev-months in detail in the next chapter). This metric, used by many publishers, tells us how much combined time is required to complete the game and the average cost of one additional month of development. This helps publishers understand how lean you are operating and approximately how much it's going to cost for every month of delay (should you require it).

---

[2] **Dev-hours** - An accounting term that refers to the total number of hours of work done by everyone on a project. Also called "man-hours."
[3] **Dev-month cost** - An accounting term that refers to the average total cost per month of development. Also called "man-month cost."

BUDGETING FOR YOUR FIRST PROJECT

The "Sample - First Project without Funding" budget represents a hypothetical group of four people who are planning to eventually begin work full-time as founders of a new studio. They represent the following roles:

- Creative Lead
- Technical Lead
- Art Lead
- Animation Lead - Starting work on the game in month seven, but helping the rest of the team out as needed on organizational matters.

Prior to starting work on their game, these individuals decided they value their work at $30,000 per year. However, with no funding coming in for this startup business, team members are doing double duty, working paying full-time jobs during the day and developing this game at night and on weekends. They opt not to take a salary.

The team recognizes the importance of including their labor in the budget. This will help set the stage for future budgeting conversations, when there is money to pay founding staff.

The budget breaks out cash expenses that must be paid from the founder salaries, which will be reimbursed later. This allows us to track the foregone compensation (the money that staff would have earned if drawing a salary) while still removing it from the running monthly cash flow at the bottom of the spreadsheet.

Thinking ahead, the team decides that should this game become successful, the founders will be paid back as revenue starts to come in after launch. Once able, the team members will start drawing a regular salary at a re-negotiated annual level. The four also agree (with the assistance of an attorney) to evenly split equity in the corporation they will form should the game find success.

The four decide that once their game reaches the alpha stage, they will have saved enough to quit their day jobs and work full-time on the project. Quitting a job that pays you well to follow your dream is a risky endeavor. We strongly urge that you consult your attorney, accountant, and, if applicable, significant other before making such a drastic change. This requires subsisting on savings while paying out-of-pocket expenses, and we recognize that this is a risk that some people simply cannot take on.

Additionally, this team recognizes the need for a business manager. They have identified someone they'd like to hire, should this game be successful enough to launch the studio. For this project, the business manager is working 20 hours per month until beta, at which time they double their commitment to see the game through launch.

In our example, the business manager will be considered a studio founder and entitled to 10 percent equity in the business, with the remaining 90 percent split among the four creative founders equally. The business manager will also be part of the reimbursement plan agreed upon by the founders.

The founders decide that in order to finish the game in a timely fashion, they will need to enlist the help of contractors. On the budget sample, these are:

- A coder
- A concept artist
- A character artist
- An environment artist

As you look at the budget, you might be wondering why contractors are making a higher hourly wage than the founders. First, contractors are always likely to be paid a higher hourly fee, as they need to pay their own taxes and supply their own tools. Second, our founders are assigning as low a value as is reasonable to their work, with the understanding that the **equity**[4] they will own in the company later will make up the difference. It is typical that founders take less up front in service of greater earnings later, once the company is successful.

The founders also determine they will need to contract sound engineering and testing at a fixed rate. Music is a trickier subject, as it can be extremely expensive. There are multiple ways to approach paying for music:

- Up-front payment. This is typically out of reach for most small teams, as music can cost hundreds of $/£/€ per minute. Depending on the composer, you can negotiate different rates to completely own the rights or simply have exclusive license for interactive media.

---

[4] **Equity** - This term has a variety of meanings depending on context. For our purposes, we are referring to "shareholder equity," which is the portion of a company owned by stockholders.

- Royalties. If you can't afford up-front payment, but want bespoke music for your game, you can negotiate a royalty fee.

- Licensing. Popular music is likely going to be far too expensive, but you may be able to find already-written (lesser known) works you want to use. Composers may be open to letting you use the music they've already created for the right price. Composers may also write bespoke music for you, but negotiate deals that allow them to retain ownership while providing an irrevocable license for specific purposes.

YOU CAN READ MORE ABOUT WORKING WITH COMPOSERS AND MUSIC LICENSING IN CHAPTER 5.

In the case of this example, the team negotiates a five percent royalty for the composer. Therefore, there are no out of pocket costs factored into the budget. The composer will start receiving payments after the game goes on sale (and platform holders begin disbursing revenue to the founders).

Other general and administrative expenses included in this sample are software as a service (SaaS) fees and property rental. For our purposes, we are including engine fees, creative tool fees, and communication tool fees. The engine and creative tool fees are assigned to employees only. Contractors would be expected to incur those costs directly (we'll talk more about employment issues in Chapter 3). The company can pay the fees related to firm-wide communication tools like Slack, which charges per-user for premium services.

The rental option we include in the budget represents working remotely or from one of the founders' homes. Later, we suggest how you might find affordable space in an office environment. However, if you continue to work remotely after forming your business, you may want to speak to an accountant about taking a business deduction for the space in your home.

We've also factored in a variety of administrative professional services. For the purposes of this example, we assume the team enlists an accountant to help with filing business taxes. We also include attorney fees to cover drafting contractor agreements and reviewing those received from contracted service providers (like the musician and sound engineer).

Travel is factored on $1,500 per person for GDC, PAX East, E3, and PAX West. These are merely used as examples, as there are now numerous regional conferences globally and the cost of attending (ticket, flight, hotel) can fluctuate wildly. Finally, we include a nominal miscellaneous budget of $200 per month for unanticipated expenses. No, it isn't much, but the team's first game is likely to be developed on a shoestring.

As you look at this sample, you'll notice two things. First, the timeline is relatively aggressive. This is simply for the sake of presenting the concepts in a digestible format.

Since this team is working on the off-hours, it will be harder to consistently come home from work just to start work on something else. That means development could be stretched further, possibly over four or five years instead of eighteen to twenty-four months.

Because we've included salary valuations for the core team, the budget for this game exceeds $300,000. Yes, that's quite high for a first project. As stated earlier, we believe it is important to recognize that time and work has value, even if you can't compensate yourself from the outset. The cash part of the budget is also significant, at over $110,000. While this team chose to hire contractors, you may choose to take on additional production roles yourselves.

You may also be able to work out arrangements with your contractors that give them a royalty on the back end (after the game starts earning money) rather than up-front payment for their services. Just remember that people die of "exposure." You can't buy food with it, and you can't pay your rent with a name in the credits of an unfinished project.

You also want to make sure you aren't giving away too much on the back end. If you "save" too much money up front by using the royalty option, you'll erode your recurring cash flow for the longer term. This will make it harder to sustain your team with revenue from game sales.

Once you do finish your game and get it onto digital marketplaces, it's time to start thinking about what's next. Our second budget can help when you're ready to start seeking funding from publishers.

BUILDING A BUDGET FOR A PUBLISHER

Our team of scrappy developers shipped their game, impressed reviewers, and found success with gamers. The studio has been incorporated and, after a brief holiday, the team put together a prototype.

Our creative lead and business manager met with publishers to pitch the game while the first project continued to earn the company revenue. After some months of negotiations, the deal has been signed and our studio's second game is now a fully-funded partnership with a small publisher.

In our second project budget, "Sample - First Project with Funding," we've added the concept of milestone payments. No longer will our team of founders be paying out of pocket. The company is a separate entity, responsible for its own financial obligations.

Despite the success, this is still a relatively small project. The team is still being frugal. Instead of an office, the five founders have decided on a co-working space with shared resources. Travel budgets are still reasonable, with the publisher providing booth and meeting space at trade and fan shows.

The big change in this budget is in the cash flow section at the bottom. Publisher disbursements are released when the team hits various milestones. We've allotted additional time for that revenue to arrive, as payment can take 30 to 45 days from invoice receipt.

With the monthly cash flow tracking, you can see how reserves are depleted monthly, only to be replenished as milestones are met. Managing cash flow can be the difference between paying your staff and destroying morale by missing a payday.

Note that these project budgets do not represent your organization's full accounting needs (for that, we encourage you to enlist the services of a licensed accountant). We'll be focusing on project budgets in this book, rather than putting together a full organizational financial profile.

Even as you move onto your second project, you are still realizing the revenue from the first game, paying back delayed salaries, and possibly investing in additional patching and bug fixes. Later on, you'll

have multiple, larger projects running at the same time. You'll also have bigger and more complex budgets...

GOING BIGGER

The final sample budget, "Sample - Later Project w Significant Funding," represents a multi-million dollar game funded by a publisher. While the scale is drastically increased from the first funded project, the concepts are the same.

To be clear, what has been provided are project budget samples and not studio budget samples. At this scale of millions of $/£/€, you (or your business partner) should be utilizing your accounting software's budgeting tools to track your project costs as well as your company costs. The project budget does not include some big ticket items like insurance or recognition of additional revenue from previous projects or debts.

Here, you'll see more employees, more contractors, greater administrative costs, and a longer timeline. You'll also see the same approach to budget planning, dev-months, and cash flow management. Once you understand the concepts of budgeting, it becomes much easier to scale up or down for different projects.

IN THIS CHAPTER, WE LEARNED....

I.   Why budgets and cash flows are important (and how they differ).
2.   How to approach your first budget, when you have no funding.
3.   How to prepare a budget that includes publisher funding.

CHAPTER
TWO

HOW MUCH IS MY PROJECT GOING TO COST EACH MONTH?

There are few inevitabilities when developing a video game. One you can almost certainly rely on is that your project will take longer and cost more than you anticipate.

In this chapter, we'll talk about how to quantify your average monthly cost, plan for overruns, and ensure that delays don't sink your project and your studio. This all begins with understanding how to build overages[1] into your budget.

---

[1] **Overage** - This is exactly what you might expect: an amount in excess of your anticipated

THE 20 PERCENT RULE

Rookie budgeters often make the same mistake when preparing their first budgets. They are honest with themselves about costs, but not time. The goal of budgeting isn't to create the lowest **bottom-line**[2] number. It's to create a document that realistically accounts for your ideal development scenario and then assumes there will be stumbles, hiccups and maybe a couple face plants along the way.

Don't feel bad. Nearly every game encounters unexpected trouble.

Staff leave, tools break or are realized to be inadequate, key features are harder to implement than anticipated, and sometimes your office gets flooded, forcing a full work stoppage. (That last one isn't common, but you should keep that kind of catastrophe in the back of your head when deciding whether your business needs insurance and devising a data backup strategy.)

In order to account for any likely (or unlikely) work interruption or slowdown, you should add 20 percent to your anticipated costs. There are two approaches to this.

If your budget is simply a list of costs for each of your departments/project roles (art, sound, coding, QA, PR, Marketing, etc.), simply add 20 percent to each line (quickest way: multiply by 1.2).

However, you might be using a budget template (like the one included in this book's digital supplement) that more closely accounts for project timing. If that's the case, you should anticipate salary, contractor fees, and professional fees at the highest end of the range. You should also consider adding additional months for task completion. For instance, if a project is expected to take five months of a contractor's time, add a one-month (20 percent) buffer in anticipation of revisions and other requirements for extension.

Some experts suggest even more conservative budgeting. If you are extremely risk-averse, like developer and industry consultant Ella Romanos, you might consider a larger buffer. "I am the world's biggest pessimist. I would probably say 25 percent," she muses.

[2] **Bottom-line** - The total cost of a project.

The result is a budget that will more closely model real costs and timeline. In many cases, this will be enough to avoid financial fallout from any potentially disastrous surprises. It will also give you a sense for cash-flow timing and your average monthly cost (also known as a "dev-month").

THE DEV-MONTH: DEFINING GAMING'S MOST ELUSIVE TERM

The bottom-line budget figure is an important piece of any financial discussion. Once you get past that point, publishers want to know how efficiently you'll run the project.

This is typically expressed as the "dev-month" cost (you may also hear the term "man-month"). This is derived from a calculation of "dev-hours" (again, you may hear the term "man-hours") that accumulates the total amount of time spent on a project by all involved.

Here's how we explain it in *The GameDev Business Handbook*:

We begin with a calculation of hours worked per month for a full-time employee.

40 hours per week x 52 weeks = 2080 dev-hours per year
2080 dev-hours per year / 12 months = 174 dev-hours per month
(rounded up)

While no employee works the full 52 weeks, you do need to pay them for the entire year. For instance, if your art team of two people each works for two years, the total number of art team dev-hours is eight-thousand three hundred fifty-two.

Art staff x Dev-hours per month x Months in two years
-or-
2 x 174 x 24 = 8,352

We use a 40 hour per week calculation for standardization purposes, even though we are aware many developers work more than that.

Dev-hours are a valuable basis for comparing scale, scope, and cost of different projects.

Dev-months are an important metric for measuring your project's viability. In order to calculate it, you'll need the total project budget and the total number of dev-hours. Divide the total dev-hours by 174 for the total number of dev-months. Then, divide the total budget by the number of dev-months to determine your average cost per month.

For instance, assume your total dev-hour count is 23,500 across all departments. We divide that by 174 to determine that we require 135.05 dev-months. We then divide our project cost (hypothetically, $700,000) by the number of dev-months, giving us a monthly average project cost of $5,183.

While the 174 hour calculation is a good place to start, there is a lack of standardization within the industry. Different publishers will use different dev-hour-per-month figures. When working with a publisher, it's important to ask for guidance on how they make their dev-month cost calculations.

In the absence of publisher guidance, we feel that the 174 hours-per-month figure is conservative. It most closely reflects costs associated with a full-time employee and a full month of work (regardless of employment status). Regional differences might be one reason publishers choose to use different hour-per-month calculations.

There's also the outdated assumption that a AAA dev-month should always cost $10,000. Even at AAA scale, there is no cookie cutter or one-size-fits-all solution for monthly costs. Geography, genre, feature set, and other factors all contribute to what a publisher will consider an acceptable dev-month cost.

Your budget isn't simply about your total expected costs. Your financial reasoning must have basis in reality. If you're asking someone else to pay for your project, you're eventually going to need to show your work and justify all of your costs. It's not enough to say that your art budget is $50,000. You'll need to explain how many people are involved, how you'll be engaging them (employee or contractor), and how long they'll be working on the project. Be prepared to explain how each item contributes to realizing your game's vision.

A **top-level budget**[3] might get you to the negotiating table, but if you can't justify your expenses, it's going to be a hard road. Either you're going to underestimate your costs (and run into trouble later) or price yourself out of a publishing deal.

The dev-month cost gives you a good idea of your efficiency and project management capabilities. It's a framework for how the project will roll out financially. If you're seeking external funding, you'll need to explain how you derived your dev-month cost, which some consider a bounding box for costs.

"I like to look at it as a sandbox," says Remedy financial controller Niko Stark. "You want to give your kids the size of the sandbox, the tools at their disposal and some reference for the sandcastle that you want them to build, as well as the time that they have to play in the sandbox. So dev-months are definitely used in ballparking budgetary numbers, but it's not the whole truth. It's very easy, but it also can be misleading if you do not understand that it is being used as a ballpark figure. You have to be careful with the dev-months. It's a very useful number, but if you use it for anything but pitching your budget to a stakeholder or a publisher, you'll need to explain it."

WHAT DO PUBLISHERS LOOK FOR WHEN EVALUATING YOUR BUDGET?

Even if your prototype is a winner and you hit it off with a publisher, you can't consider a deal in the bag until you get past the budget discussion. Even if your game sounds like a sure thing, publishers need to feel confident that you can accomplish your goals at a reasonable cost.

---

[3] **Top-level budget** - This is a simplified budget that breaks down major cost areas without overwhelming the reader with every single line item. This budget might include only a few line items for key production concerns like art, sound, coding, QA, marketing and PR, overhead, and other major expenses.

Every publisher looks at budgets differently, and every developer has its own way of working. Devolver Digital (*Hotline Miami, Enter the Gungeon*) producer Andrew Parsons says there are key factors he looks for when reviewing a production budget.

"These include things like the amount of money versus the scope of the game, timing and delivery of payments, and hotspots and gaps in the schedule," he explains. "There is a range of aspects to it and they all work in harmony with each other. When it comes down to it, it's not an exact science, and a lot of my time is spent just asking people, 'What do you think you need?' and using that as a starting point for what they actually do. The game must have defined start and end points, there must be defined production deliverables—i.e. Alpha, Beta, Gold Master—and then we need the average **burn rate**[4] of the studio—i.e. how much a 'normal' staff cost is. As each game is different the must-haves can change quite a bit."

On the flip side, publishers are keenly aware that developers often mistakenly try to lowball projects. You might think that cutting your costs on paper is going to woo a publisher, but you likely won't fool anyone. Even if a publisher doesn't realize your costs are unrealistically low, you'll pay for it later when you inevitably run over budget. Making an unfounded point about affordability can lead you down the path of ruin.

---

[4] **Burn rate** - The pace at which a company spends money, often in excess of income.

"My job is to help devs understand that they need to be more realistic with their requirements and think carefully about what that means for both us and them," Parsons says. "A few other things that we'll look for are production-related areas that tend to have their own associated costs. Simple questions like, 'What engine does the game use?', 'How much text are you planning to write?', and, 'How many languages are you supporting?' can yield some useful answers when it comes to topping up a budget."

THE ART OF BUDGET EVALUATION AND THE VALUE OF CANCELING PROJECTS

There is an art to budget and project evaluation, too. It's not enough to have a good game that's technically solid and enjoyable to play. You need to know where the market is right now and prognosticate about where it will be when your game is expected to launch.

"It's divided between art, science and tech, and then just market research," says Remedy executive producer Tuukka Taipalvesi. "With our dev cycles, which are years and not months, we need to try to see the future to a degree. What are the types of games that we want to make, and where is the market going in the space where we want to be? There's been a lot of talk about long, single-player games not being financially feasible anymore. That's what we have been doing for tens of years: single-player, story driven, narrative games that have high production values are not the cheapest things to produce. They don't have as much repeat play value as some other titles out there have, so we need to take all of this into account when we actually start new projects in this climate."

The debate on whether video games are art is long settled. (They are. They're also commercial. It's OK. They can be both.)

It's the artistic piece of the puzzle that makes it hardest to predict a game's success. Even if we had a crystal ball that gave us perfect market foresight, it wouldn't be the only challenging piece of the predictive model.

We can't perfectly predict trends, and consumers continue to surprise us as they gather around games that seemingly emerged out of nowhere (see Chapter 8 for more on the romantic notion of the "overnight success"). That means developers and publishers need to stay vigilant throughout a project.

"The market is constantly in flux. It's always going to be a calculated risk in order to determine the feasibility of a project," Taipalvesi says. "You don't determine feasibility when you start. You determine that milestone by milestone. You need to be able to say to yourself, 'This isn't working. We need to cancel and move on as soon as possible.' Like Supercell (*Clash of Clans, Clash Royale*) **has been saying**[5] for years and years, you need to fail early. You need to fail often, and you need to fail as early as you can so you can lose the least amount of money from your failures. But you also need to learn from the failures. It's as much art as it is science, and it's a very difficult problem to solve. That's why gaming companies rise and fall left and right."

HOW DOES DEV-MONTH COST PLAY INTO PUBLISHER FUNDING?

Publishers are often exceedingly risk-sensitive, especially as budgets grow and the market becomes more hit-driven. Paradox Interactive (*Europa Universalis, Crusader Kings, Surviving Mars*), for example, uses a number of risk-related criteria to determine whether it wants to invest in a game. These include:

- Project viability: Will the game likely be enjoyable to play?
- Team: Who is making the game? Do they have the experience and skill to execute on the vision?
- Paradox's own capacity: Can Paradox support the game's vision to make it a success in the market?
- Market impact: Does this game appeal to a significant portion of the market when compared against its budget?
- Current player base: Does this game fit our portfolio and existing (or desired) audience profile?

"The analysis is comprised of a mix of qualitative—experience and gut feeling—and quantitative data—public sales figures, our sales data, and other reports," says Paradox vice president of business development Shams Jorjani. "At this point we'll have some basic projections in place telling us the worst case, realistic case, and

[5] Samantha Murphy. "Gaming Empire Supercell: We Pop Champagne Every Time We Fail," *Mashable*. November 13, 2013. https://mashable.com/2013/11/13/supercell-apps-success/#icCpuUP3sOqM. (accessed February 27, 2018).

optimistic case. The last one we just throw out right away. We just double check that there is a breakout potential. Then we sober up and end up basing the business case on an estimate somewhere between worst case and realistic, but closer to the latter. We have fairly high requirements for return on investment, and if everything holds up, we proceed. We're basically saying that things can go slightly wrong and we should still be making money to be able to keep going in the long term."

Paradox also looks at a game's genre to help determine feasibility. Grand strategy, first-person shooters, MMOs, and adventure games all have different reasonable budgets and sales potential.

"Different types of games require different resources," Jorjani explains. "A system-heavy game will naturally require a lot of engineering work over a longer period of time. Art is much easier to outsource for much lower costs. Another impact is when costs occur. Having a big art budget for outsourcing is one thing - it's another matter when in the development timeline it's being spent. There's also the factor that different genres have different sales potential. It's fine to spend more if the maximum potential of the game is greater."

Spending money as late in the development cycle as is feasible helps to limit wasted work. It's important to engage your contractors when you can give them clear guidance on your vision and expectations. For example, tasking an environment artist too early might lead to work that can't be used if the overall aesthetic changes later.

In addition, Paradox hunts for red flags in the budget and planning documents. These include:

- Overly optimistic sales expectations.
- A lack of contingency planning related to timeline.
- Missing outsourcing details.
- Few details and explanation related to design choices.

Dev-month cost factors into this analysis, as it takes operational factors into consideration. These include team size and geography. Jorjani spoke at length about dev-month costs on a **December 2017 Paradox**[6] podcast with the company's communications and content manager, Daniel Goldberg.

---

[6] Shams Jorjani and Daniel Goldberg, The Paradox Podcast, podcast audio, December 4, 2017, https://soundcloud.com/user-47372246/the-paradox-podcast-s01e05-what-does-it-cost-to-make-a-video-game.

What we see when people approach us are rates that range anywhere from €3,000 to €15,000 per month, as an average across the entire team. That's a massive difference. That's not just salary. It covers all the social costs, the costs of running the business, keeping the lamps on, toilet paper, heating, internet bills, etc. Everything should be covered by that expense. You take all your expenses and divide that by the number of people you have in the company, and that's your man-month.

€3,000 would be a developer that has a base of operations in a small town and very low overhead. Maybe everyone is working from home. They may be in a country that has tax incentives. We also talk about young folks without families or dependents. It's on the very low end of the spectrum. In Sweden, we have relatively high social costs. €4,000, for instance, the actual salary would be something like €2,500. That's roughly on par with lower paying jobs. You're paying a social fee, but that doesn't cover any of the costs of running the actual business.

When we talk about established developers, with long track records, likely with bigger overhead and located in expensive locations like London or Stockholm, they charge anywhere from €12,000 to €15,000 per man-month. It can be even higher. We're talking about people who are very experienced in their field, very competitive, and very successful.

Consultant and developer Ella Romanos agrees that a variety of factors play into budget evaluation. "I think geography of the studio makes a huge difference. Even within a country, salaries vary hugely," she explains, speaking about the United Kingdom. "A studio in Guildford will have salary rates hugely higher than a studio in, say, Cornwall. So I will definitely take into account the geography. Then I'll also consider the length of the project. If it's a big project, I would probably expect profit margins to be a bit lower than on smaller and shorter projects."

"The experience of the team is going to matter because they are going to be paid more," Romanos continued. "So that would be taken into account, as will the type of project. You wouldn't be talking to a team who couldn't do it. If you're doing something that's very technically challenging, then you'd probably be talking to a more experienced team or one with specific skills, and, therefore, you would expect to pay more."

A team's track record is also important because of resources the studio is able to contribute in case of a massive, unanticipated hitch

in development. Having existing revenue streams to help support current development can give a publisher confidence.

"There's a big difference in a studio with low costs and no other revenue streams and an established studio with high costs but many other clients/revenue streams," Jorjani says. "If—when—a project falls behind and somebody has to foot the bill, working with a less expensive developer isn't going to be of much help because the publisher must cover costs. If it's a professional outfit with money in the bank, they're going to honor their commitment and pay out of pocket to deliver what they promised."

WHAT DOES IT MEAN IF YOUR DEV-MONTH COST IS TOO HIGH OR TOO LOW?

Ultimately, there is no "right" dev-month cost. Finding your budgeting sweet spot is a combination of factors, including team size, experience, overhead, geography, game genre, and (most importantly) the requirements to execute on your vision. Along the way, you may need to scale back your design goals for the sake of feasibility. If you can do this without sacrificing your artistic intent, the way forward could illuminate.

If you can't, it might be time to shelve your project for another time. It's important to see the value in prototyping. It isn't just about finding ideas that work, it's about realistically identifying those that don't.

"Often, games get canceled," Jorjani said on the December 4, 2017 Paradox Podcast. "They don't pan out or you start off by creating a number of proofs of concepts and prototypes. You have a mechanic you want to try out. There's a lot of research and development that goes into making games."

If your dev-month cost is too high (either for your own tolerance or for publishers to take a chance), it's important to revisit your costs.

- Are you spending too much on **overhead**[7]?
- Are you planning on hiring more people than you can reasonably sustain?
- Can you use contractors instead? (More on this in Chapter 3)
- Does your budget call for tool creation when there are reasonable engines and middleware options already available?
- Are you planning too much time for development compared to the project scale and market viability?

Likewise, publishers can have concerns about dev-month costs that are too low. Most often, this means the developer hasn't fully considered (or included) some key costs.

When looking at a budget that seems unreasonably low, publishers and financers will often be warned off as timelines and costs are likely to grow at unexpected points during development. Ensuring that you've accounted for every cost category is important. Forgetting categories or, worse, hiding costs can put off a potential partner.

"People tend to actually try to push the budget down as much as possible, and sometimes to the point where it's concerning," Romanos says. "So, asking for too little is as much of a concern as asking for too much. To check that the budget looks sensible, I would look at the details and check that it looks reasonable in terms of salary particularly. Are they going to be out to hire people who are experienced enough to be able to deliver a project reliably? For example, if all the salaries are showing really low, I would wonder if they're going to hire a group of graduates, and that would worry me."

---

[7] **Overhead** - Costs related to rent, utilities, accounting, legal, interest expense, taxes, and more that exist independent of development.

Budget with honesty. Don't try to sugarcoat your numbers. If they seem too high, refine and revise without sacrificing your vision. If you can't bring the numbers in line with your development goals, it might be time to move on to other ideas.

SOME PUBLISHERS DON'T RELY ON DEV-MONTHS

While dev-month cost is a common way of evaluating project efficiency and feasibility, it isn't used universally. Devolver Digital's Andrew Parsons suggests that dev-months aren't always valuable for teams working on their first project.

"I don't believe there's a great deal of mileage in that, especially with those less-experienced developers," Parsons says. "It all comes down to the mercurial nature of game design and development."

He believes that time estimates are easier for some tasks than others. Because of variability and the inherent uncertainty of the design process, Parsons prefers to use a different methodology.

"The risk of slippage (and thus changing costs) is so great that we find it's better to suggest that developers be flexible in their task scheduling rather than trying to fix them in stone," he explains. "Experience also plays a huge role in this. If you've been doing this for years, then you'll know what an estimate looks like for this system or that piece of art, but if it's literally the first time you've done that work, how do you know how long it takes? Once you combine that with the fact that most developers hate being challenged about their time estimates, you're staring at a pretty non-scientific approach."

Devolver takes a much more fluid approach to developer costs, because it doesn't live and die by the dev-month approach. Because of the relationships the publisher builds with its partners, relationship is a big piece of the budgeting puzzle.

"Our approach is normally based on, 'What do you need to do the best job you can do without distraction?' rather than, 'We need for you to come in cheap,'" Parsons says. "I'm sure that there's a solution to this, but as a publisher, our job is to support the developer in their endeavor and help them understand the business side of making games. Who am I to point at a schedule and say, 'I believe you need to hire more artists, because I can't believe it's going to take you three days to create that mesh or animate that sprite.' I mean, I have a rough idea, but every developer is different so it's only ever an idea."

WHAT HAPPENS WHEN A DELAY OR BUDGET OVERRUN IS MORE SIGNIFICANT THAN YOU LEFT ROOM FOR?

Chances are, your game is going to take longer in development than you anticipate. If you accounted for an additional 20 percent in your timeline and budget, you might be just fine.

Sometimes though, the delay you're considering will cost more than your conservative budgeting allows for. In that case, you'll need to make some hard decisions.

First, evaluate how important the delay is to meeting your goals. In some cases, technical issues or challenges implementing key differentiating features might simply be harder than anticipated. In these cases, you might have no choice. However, if the delay isn't in service of releasing a viable product or won't make a significant impact on sales, you may choose to alter your vision rather than your development timeline.

When you're working independently, this means looking at your personal finances and your studio's financial health. You'll need to ensure you have the cash on hand to continue paying staff and contractors until the game ships.

If you're working with a publisher, major delays and budget overruns can have long-term impact. If you can't fill in the budget overrun from your studio's coffers, you'll need to ask your publisher for additional funding.

This will likely trigger a contract renegotiation in which you'll likely have to give something up, including any combination of:

- **Revenue share points:** This could lead to a potentially severe impairment to long-term revenue on the project, which ultimately hinders your company's future prospects.

- **The intellectual property:** If it's owned by the developer, the publisher might offer to purchase the property in exchange for more funding.

- **The relationship:** The publisher might cancel the contract and hand the already-completed work to another studio. The project could also be canceled outright.

Exercise conservative budgeting (and leave yourself a 20 to 25 percent buffer). Ensure that you aren't lowballing the project cost. Find the middle ground and you may be saving yourself from an uncomfortable conversation that will ultimately hurt the company's financial health.

EASILY OVERLOOKED BUDGET ITEMS

You're unlikely to forget to build art, sound, and coding into your budget. However, there are line items that might slip through the cracks, only to surprise you later as unanticipated expenditures.

USER TESTING

Quality assurance and user testing are important to refining your design and gameplay. Without them, you're working in the dark. Developers can overlook the importance of user testing as part of the budgeting process.

"I'd expect to see a user testing focus, so I would expect to see time written into any budget for testing, feedback, and iteration," says consultant and developer Ella Romanos. "We don't see that very much. It always worries me."

ACCOUNTING AND LEGAL COSTS

Running a company brings with it complicated accounting issues. Financing, payroll taxes, regional tax incentives, royalties, and licensing all complicate your accounting picture. Make sure you leave room to hire someone to help you.

"I expect realistic accountancy costs," Romanos says. "Lots of people put like £100 in for accountants. As an example, I always spread our accounting cost out over the year because, even though you actually end up paying it in one chunk, it's much easier to see it. Be pessimistic, in terms of when the money's going to go out."

The same is true of legal costs. You're going to want an attorney to draft and review contracts, especially as you seek publisher funding. Anticipating those expenses and allocating them over time will help you spend money to protect your legal rights without worry. The last thing you want is the temptation to pinch pennies when your company's financial and legal health are on the line.

MARKETING

Your game isn't going to sell itself. Discoverability on mobile, PC, and console storefronts is increasingly challenging.

It's important to build a communication profile that introduces prospective players to your game and feeds them information throughout the development cycle. It's rare, even for established developers, to find success with quiet releases.

If people don't know about your game, they can't purchase it. If they don't buy your game, you might not be able to afford to make another.

"If you aren't the publisher, then you may not be funding marketing," Romanos says. "It may not even be up to you what the publisher spends. But I think it's very unlikely, these days, that you're not going to need some kind of marketing yourself. You'll need to likely invest in community management, too. It depends on the project, but if a developer hasn't included any marketing funding, then I would want it specified why."

LOCALIZATION

If you follow developers on social media and have ever seen one desperately asking for an Arabic translation... it means they very likely missed that certain platform holders require consumer-facing store descriptions be translated into numerous languages (including Arabic). If you decide to localize your game (or even if you don't), don't forget that many platforms require localization on their stores. If your game is heading to console, be sure to ask about required languages for store metadata. Account for those costs! And please don't rely on Google Translate.

YOU CAN READ MORE ABOUT
LOCALIZATION IN CHAPTER 4.

IN THIS CHAPTER, WE LEARNED....

1. How to calculate dev-month cost.
2. Why dev-month costs are important for development planning.
3. How delays can impact your project budget and revenue share.

CHAPTER THREE

WHAT DOES IT REALLY COST TO HIRE AN EMPLOYEE?

Hidden costs are part of nearly every facet of 21st-century living. Your mobile phone bill is loaded with them. Your broadband statement is never as low as the quoted fee. And the car dealership is always trying to sneak in small expenses to balloon your dream car's cost above the price tag.

Employing staff brings with it a series of expenses that go beyond salary. It's too easy for employers and employees to focus on the number in the offer letter. However, regional laws and obligations make hiring and carrying employees more complicated

EMPLOYMENT IN THE UNITED STATES – CONTRACTORS, EMPLOYEES, AND YOU

Every region has different ways of classifying workers. In the United States, there are two main categories: employees and contractors. The federal government is particular about how you label workers, because of the differences in payment structure and tax obligation.

Companies are not required to pay taxes on behalf of contractors. They are, however, required to withhold payments from employee pay and match income tax contributions on a regular basis. Additionally, contractors are often ineligible for unemployment insurance, company health benefits, paid time off, sick leave, and other parts of the employee benefit package.

For this reason, misclassification of employees can result in severe legal consequences, including immediate back-pay and tax reimbursement. Companies found to have misclassified employees may also be subject to punitive fees. The Internal Revenue Service (IRS) uses a four-factor test to determine whether a worker should be classified as an employee or a contractor. There are some questions you can ask yourself in order to determine whether you've handled this correctly.

WILL I DICTATE WHERE THIS PERSON WORKS?

Do you require this person to be present in your office to accomplish their work? If so, they are more likely to be deemed an employee. In contrast, contractors are more likely to be able to work from home, a cafe, or anywhere else they choose.

DO I REQUIRE THIS PERSON TO WORK SPECIFIC HOURS?

If you expect someone to be at their desk from 9 am to 5 pm every day, you're dictating more of how they accomplish their job. This leans heavily toward employee status. If you're more concerned with deliverables (specific outcomes required from an employee), you likely have a contractor situation on your hands. Contractors set their own hours, work mostly independently, and have specific tasks to accomplish.

Contractors are typically only responsible for getting you the goods (concept art, score, animations, etc.) by a negotiated deadline. If someone is nocturnal, but gets you what you need on time, then you've probably engaged a contractor.

AM I EXPECTING THIS PERSON TO WORK EXCLUSIVELY FOR ME?

If the job takes up an enormous portion of a worker's time, making the case that they are a contractor will be harder. Likewise, if you demand exclusivity, you are hiring an employee. Contractors typically have multiple clients and aren't tied to a single company.

HOW LONG WILL MY RELATIONSHIP WITH THE PERSON LAST?

If you want to bring on someone for many months (or years), be careful. The longer a relationship goes on, and the more vital someone is to daily operations, the more likely they should be classified as an employee. In contrast, contractors typically work with clients for discrete periods and then move on. They may team up with you again, but each engagement is often a new contract.

WILL I BE OFFERING BENEFITS TO THIS PERSON, LIKE HEALTH INSURANCE, SICK TIME, OR PAID VACATION?

If the answer is yes, you're firmly in employee territory.

WILL I BE SUPPLYING A COMPUTER, SOFTWARE LICENSES, OR OTHER NECESSARY TOOLS?

Contractors typically provide their own equipment and tools. Employees can reasonably expect that you'll give them what they need to do their jobs. If you are providing equipment and software, you are likely working with an employee

Why are we spending so much time on this in a budgeting workbook? Because getting it wrong can obliterate your business.

Once you've determined how to classify a worker, you'll have a better sense of how to calculate your monthly costs. Contractors will charge you a flat rate for work or an hourly rate. If your partner opts to use hourly billing, it would behoove you to request an anticipated range for the time commitment. When you budget, use the top of the range and then add 20 percent as a buffer for delays and revisions.

If the worker is better classified as an employee, there are a number of considerations for determining annual cost. Much of this is pegged to salary.

Each state has its own tax code and mandatory contributions. Gusto, a human resources and payroll services provider, has conveniently aggregated **employment cost calculators**[1] for all 50 states and the District of Columbia.

The federal government gets its cut regardless of the state in which you reside. This appears on your paycheck as "FICA" (Federal Insurance Contribution Act). This represents contribution to the social security fund and Medicare. Additionally, there is federally mandated unemployment tax.

As an example, here's what it would cost to employ someone making $50,000 per year in New Jersey:

Chart 3.1 - True Cost of Hiring (New Jersey, United States example)

	Amount
Gross Salary	$50,000.00
FICA - Social Security **(6.2% of salary)**[2]	$ 3,100.00
FICA - Medicare **(1.45% of salary)**[1]	$ 725.00
Federal Unemployment Tax Act **(6% of first $7,000 wages after 5.4% credit)**[3]	$ 42.00
New Jersey Workforce Development Tax **(.1175% of first $32,600 wages)**[4]	$ 38.30
New Jersey State Disability Insurance **(.5% of first $32,600)**[3]	$ 163.00
Total Employee Annual Cost*	**$54,068.31**

[1]   "Employer tax calculator," Gusto.com. https://gusto.com/tools/employer-tax-calculator.
        (accessed March 5, 2018).
[2]   "Social Security and Medicare Withholding Rates," IRS.gov.
        https://www.irs.gov/taxtopics/tc751.html. (accessed July 4, 2017).
[3]   "Employer's Annual Federal Unemployment (FUTA) Tax Return - Filing and Deposit Requirements,"
        IRS.gov. https://www.irs.gov/taxtopics/tc759.html. (accessed July 4, 2017).
[4]   "Division of Employer Accounts 2018 Rates," State of New Jersey Department of Labor and
        Workforce Development. http://lwd.dol.state.nj.us/labor/ea/rates/ea2018.html.
        (accessed December 6, 2017).

While the tax calculators will reveal your obligation to state and federal governments, they don't fully detail your obligation to employees. As your company matures, you'll likely build a benefits package that will help attract and retain talent.

In the United States, these additional perks might include:

- Life insurance
- Long term disability insurance
- Sick leave
- Vacation days
- Personal days
- Professional development
- Retirement savings plans (which may be matched up to a certain point by the company)
- Medical insurance

The last item on the list is a big one. Medical insurance plans take time and effort to administer. Many employers cover some (often quite a lot) of plan costs. This can amount to thousands of dollars per employee every year, with rates increasing with every annual renewal.

In 2018, you should anticipate insurance costs between $5,000 and $13,000 per employee. This is dependent on geography, insurer, and changes to the law that might be enacted by the United States government.

Of course, if you happen to live in the UK, Canada, or most of the other developed nations, basic health care costs aren't a concern for employers. Though, rules around employment classification and taxation vary significantly.

WORKING IN CANADA

While there are many similarities between United States and Canadian employment law, it's important to remember that things are different north of the 49th parallel. One of the biggest differences is the American concept of **"at will"**[5] employment.

In the United States, at-will employment favors the employer's ability to make staffing changes without warning and for almost any reason. The same is not true in Canada, where employees are entitled to reasonable notice when a company decides to terminate their employment.

Employees are granted a number of protections on a province-by-province basis. These include:

- Minimum wage standards
- Work hour restrictions
- Overtime pay
- Statutory Holidays
- Vacation allowance
- Leaves of absence
- Methods and notice of termination

[5] **At-will employment** - In most of the United States, employers can dismiss employees for any reason except discrimination, whistleblowing, or exercising your legal rights (like taking family or medical leave). Contractual employment that specifies termination procedures and remedies would supercede the at-will doctrine.

Contractors are not entitled to these protections. The distinction between the two classes is handled similarly to how it is in the United States.

"The relationship between an employee and an employer is one that is viewed by courts as one where the employer has power over the employee, and each party owes duties to the other that are well-protected at law," explains lawyer Ryan Black, chief technology partner at McMillan. "The relationship between a contractor and the hiring party is one that is viewed as equals, where each party is performing in its own best interests, and courts will look to enforce the true bargain reached between them. Typically, contractual relationships are expected to be terminable in accordance with their terms—which may include immediate termination or very short notice—whereas employment relationships must be terminable in accordance with legislative minimums."

Canada courts have recently described a third worker class, the dependent contractor. This exists between employee and contractor status, typically when an independent worker derives most or all of their income from a single hiring party. "A 'dependent' contractor, like an employee, is entitled to reasonable notice of termination (presumably, regardless of what the contract says unless it would comply with employment legislative minimums)," Black explains.

The Canada Revenue Agency uses the Sagaz Test (named after a Supreme Court of Canada case) to determine whether a worker should be classified as a contractor or employee. Provincial courts, employment tribunals, and the agencies that administer the Canada Pension Plan and Employment Insurance programs may also be involved in determining classification.

"Recognizing that the terminology used in the contract itself—or what the parties consider themselves—may not be determinative, the Sagaz test attempts to answer the question by looking at the total relationship between the parties and answering the question, 'Is the worker engaged as a person in business for his or her own account, or in the business of the hiring party?' Black says. To that end, the following factors are considered:

- The control that the hiring party has over the worker and the worker's performance of activities (i.e., the independence the worker as over how the work can be done, when the work can be done and what work will be done)

- Whether the worker takes on financial risk or has an opportunity for profit
- Whether the worker can take on other work
- Whether the worker is providing services through a corporation or individually
- Whether the worker can subcontract the work, hire assistants (which, obviously, would increase the ability to have risk or profit)
- Which party provides the tools and equipment
- The responsibility for investment and management the worker has in the context of the hiring party, and
- Many other factors, including terms that appear in the employment contract.

The new "dependent contractor" status is not considered in the classification process for taxation purposes. Employers can refer to a **document published by the Canada Revenue Agency**[6] for guidance on classification matters.

Ensuring that you classify workers properly is crucial for employers. There can be severe repercussions for treating a worker as a contractor when they should have been handled as an employee.

At the bare minimum, employers would be responsible for compensating the government for all unpaid pension and employment insurance premiums. Additionally, there may be penalties for failure to properly classify. Even though there is an employer and employee piece of pay withholding for these things, the employer may be burdened with the entire amount, relieving the employee of responsibility during the period of misclassification.

"A bigger surprise may come if a contractor is an actual employee and the contract did not provide for the minimum standards of employment, such as minimum wage, overtime, leaves, notice of termination, and the like, all of which may become applicable if an employee was misclassified as a contractor," Black cautions. "A hiring party may find itself the subject of a lawsuit or tribunal claim in light of any missed standards, or for a claim for wrongful dismissal—either as a dependent contractor or as a misclassified employee—resulting in severance or pay in lieu of termination notice. Employees and employers cannot contract out of minimums that apply to employees, and cannot agree that a British Columbia employee could be hired

---

[6] "Employee or Self-Employed," Canada Revenue Agency. November 7, 2017.
     https://www. canada.ca/en/revenue-agency/services/forms-publications/publications/
     rc4110-employee-self-employed/employee-self-employed.html.
     (accessed January 4, 2018).

under, for example, Russian law and the minimum standards there. The contract as a whole will have to be re-evaluated in light of the misclassification and its implications."

Many video game firms hire within a country, but contractors can live around the world. Just be careful that you are aware of employment law in your contractor's home country.

"When you add an international border to the equation, the test of that person's jurisdiction may also apply," Black warns. "When you engage a person to work for you from a remote location, you are necessarily engaging the laws of that jurisdiction. Businesses may find themselves subject to the jurisdiction—tax or legal—of another country or province by hiring an employee or contracting internationally."

WHAT TAXES ARE CANADIAN EMPLOYERS RESPONSIBLE FOR?

If you're hiring employees in Canada, you'll be responsible for withholding a portion of their pay and forwarding that to the government. You'll also need to pay into pension and employment insurance programs.

Chart 3.2 - True Cost of Hiring (**British Columbia, Canada - 2018 example[7]**)

	Amount
Gross Salary	$60,000.00
Canada Pension Plan (CPP)	$ 2,593.80
Employment Insurance (1.4x Employee Contribution Rate)	$ 1,201.51
Total Employee Annual Cost	**$63,795.31**

[7] "Payroll Deductions Online Calculator," Canada Revenue Agency. January 1, 2018. https://apps.cra-arc.gc.ca/ebci/rhpd/wlcm-bnvn.do. (accessed January 4, 2018).

"Many employers provide for an extended benefits program, and the costs of these must be weighed by the typical startup business against the benefit to employee health, happiness and retention," says lawyer Mike Reid, co-chair of McMillan's startups and emerging companies group. Additional benefits (including those required by law) might include:

- Vacation time
- Sick time
- Employee assistance programs
- Disability insurance
- Worker's compensation (for some employers)
- Medical and family leave
- Extended health care (including prescription coverage, dental care,and eye care)
- Personal days

Note that the Canada Revenue Agency calculator is a good resource for every province except Québec, which **offers its own solution.**[8]

If you are a contractor, you'll need to pay taxes directly to the government. In addition, you will likely need to charge the hiring company a goods and services tax. The following chart is an example of how this tax impacts contractor invoicing.

*Chart 3.3 - Goods and Services Tax for Contractors (**British Columbia, Canada - 2018 example**[9])*

	Amount
Invoice Amount	$ 5,000.00
Goods and Services Tax (5%)	$ 250.00
Provincial Sales Tax (7%)	$ 350.00
Total Employee Annual Cost	**$ 5,600.00**

---

[8] "WINRAS - Calculation of Source Deductions and Employer Contributions," Revenu Québec. http://www.revenuquebec.ca/en/sepf/services/sgp_winras/default.aspx. (accessed January 5, 2018).

[9] "GST/HST Calculator (and rates)," Canada Revenue Agency. http://www.cra-arc.gc.ca/tx/bsnss/tpcs/gst-tps/rts-eng.html#rt. (accessed January 4, 2018).

GET SMART ABOUT TAX CREDITS

Many countries and regions offer tax credits for specific work. In the UK, the Video Game Tax Relief helps with production taking place in that country (more on this below). Canadians can also access a variety of tax credits. Each comes with specific requirements that must be carefully navigated to maintain eligibility.

Lawyer Michel Ranger, tax partner at McMillan, explains what you should consider when pursuing tax credits for video game and development tool creation.

There are complicated implications. For example, for businesses trying to claim Scientific Research and Experimental Development tax credits, which are available to businesses that conduct research and development in respect of new, improved, or technologically advanced products or processes—and may certainly be claimed by certain video game technology companies—having a true independent contractor conduct that work may affect the ability of the business trying to claim that credit. Certainly, before relying upon a certain amount of tax credits being available, or applying for such credits with the appropriate federal and provincial tax authorities, your tax and legal advisors would want to understand your workforce and how it is comprised in order to assess the extent of their availability.

Be sure to carefully read all of the material on tax relief initiatives before counting them in your budget. Ask your legal and financial advisors for assistance in determining eligibility.

WORKING IN THE UK

The UK has similar classifications to the United States and Canada, with core groups called "employed" and "self-employed." The latter is similar to the "contractor" designation in the United States and Canada. Additionally, directors and office holders (e.g. President of the Board of Directors) have their own classification which can be held contemporaneously with employment status.

Additionally, there is a "worker" designation that is similar to Canada's "dependent contractor" status. Her Majesty's Revenue & Customs (HMRC) offers a **self-administered classification tool**[10] that employers should use when determining how to treat a relationship.

"A reference is provided at the end of the tool and HMRC will stand by the result given unless a compliance check finds the information provided isn't accurate," says accountant Nick Johnson, managing director of Affect Group. Johnson provides the following table of conditions and rights that helps define the classifications, while detailing the rights to which each group is entitled.

---

[10] "Check employment status for tax," Her Majesty's Revenue and Customs.
https://www.tax.service.gov.uk/check-employment-status-for-tax/setup.
(accessed January 17, 2018).

Chart 3.4 - UK Worker classifications

Classification	Conditions	Rights
Employee	1. Required to work regularly unless they're on leave 2. Required to do a minimum number of hours and expect to be paid for time worked 3. Get paid holiday 4. Entitled to contractual or Statutory Sick Pay, and maternity or paternity pay 5. Can join the business's pension scheme 6. Work at the business's premises or at an address specified by the business 7. Business provides the materials, tools and equipment for their work 8. Only work for the business or if they do have another job, it's completely different from their work for the business	1. Statutory Sick Pay 2. Statutory maternity, paternity, adoption and shared parental leave and pay (workers only get pay, not leave) 3. Minimum notice periods if their employment will be ending, for example if an employer is dismissing them 4. Protection against unfair dismissal 5. Right to request flexible working 6. Time off for emergencies 7. Statutory Redundancy Pay
Self-Employed	1. Individual is in business for themselves, are responsible for the success or failure of their business and can make a loss or a profit	1. Rights and responsibilities are set out by the terms of the contract they have with their client

Classification	Conditions	Rights
Self-Employed	2. Can decide what work they do and when, where or how to do it 3. Can hire someone else to do the work 4. Are responsible for fixing any unsatisfactory work in their own time their employer agrees a fixed price for their work - it doesn't depend on how long the job takes to finish 5. Use own money to buy business assets, cover running costs, and provide tools and equipment for their work 6. Generally work for more than one client	
Worker	1. Have a contract or other arrangement to do work or services personally for a reward (your contract doesn't have to be written) 2. Reward is for money or a benefit in kind, for example the promise of a contract or future work 3. Only have a limited right to send someone else to do the work (subcontract)	1. National Minimum Wage 2. Protection against unlawful deductions from wages 3. Statutory minimum level of paid holiday 4. Statutory minimum length of rest breaks 5. Right to not work more than 48 hours on average per week or to opt out of this right if they choose 6. Protection against unlawful discrimination

Classification	Conditions	Rights
Worker	4. Have to turn up for work even if they don't want to 5. Their employer has to have work for them to do as long as the contract or arrangement lasts 6. Not doing the work as part of their own limited company in an arrangement where the 'employer' is actually a customer or client	7. Right to not be treated less favourably if they work part-time 8. Normally statutory sick pay, maternity, paternity and adoption pay
Director/Officer (may also be employee)	1. No contract or service agreement relating to their appointment 2. Duties are minimal, and are only those required under the relevant statute, constitution or trust deed 3. Don't get a salary or any other form of regular payment for their services 4. Only payment they get is a voluntary payment (honorarium), regardless of the work they do - tax and National Insurance are deducted by the appointing body 5. Effectively working as an independent office, and are not under the close supervision or control of the appointing body	1. Voting on company business 2. If also an employee, have rights as such

Classifications can be complicated by additional factors. For instance, an individual might perform work through an intermediary (like a personal service company) but would otherwise be classified as an employee if they had contracted individually. In cases such as these, taxation rules may require an accountant's assistance. It is far better to pay for help than to make a costly error.

"Where an individual is an employee, the company will pay Class 1 National Insurance which is generally 12.8 percent of the salary plus a pension contribution," Johnson explains. "UK employers are generally required to contribute to the individual's pension. There are no other compulsory benefits to all employers but there are some stringent health and safety requirements which may lead to free eye tests for people using computers a lot of the time."

Self-employed individuals are responsible for remitting their own taxes to HMRC. The following calculator demonstrates what employers should expect for carrying an employee:

Chart 3.5 - *True Cost of Hiring (UK)*[11]

	Amount
Gross Salary	£50,000.00
Employer National Insurance Contribution (11.54674 percent)	£ 5,773.37
Pension Contribution (5 percent)	£ 2,500.00
Total Employee Annual Cost	**£58,273.37**

[11] "UK Tax Calculator," ListenToTaxMan.com.
https://listentotaxman.com/50000?yr=2018&pension=0.
(accessed January 17, 2018).

Additionally, employers are responsible for withholding a portion of an employee's pay for tax purposes. In the UK, the **tax rates**[12] are applied in a tiered structure. The first £11,850 you earn will not be taxed. Earnings between £11,851 and £33,500 are subject to a 20 percent tax rate.

Income between £33,501 and £150,000 are taxed at 40 percent. Anything above that is taxed at 45 percent.

As an employer, misclassification can be costly. If HMRC determines you have misclassified someone, you'll be responsible for additional tax and national insurance, as well as interest. HMRC will assess the severity of the misclassification and your actions related to it, with the following additional penalties on top of repayment of owed funds.

Chart 3.6 - HMRC penalties for worker misclassification

Type of behaviour	Unprompted disclosure	Prompted disclosure
Reasonable care	No penalty	No penalty
Careless	0% to 30%	15% to 30%
Deliberate	20% to 70%	35% to 70%
Deliberate and concealed	30% to 100%	50% to 100%

12 "Annex A: rates and allowances," Her Majesty's Revenue and Customs. November 22, 2017. https://www.gov.uk/government/publications/autumn-budget-2017-overview-of-tax-legislation-and-rates-ootlar/annex-a-rates-and-allowances. (accessed January 17, 2018).

HIRING NON-RESIDENTS TO WORK FOR YOUR STUDIO

Your search for talent might take you to far-off lands. If the perfect fit for your studio is a citizen of another country, things are going to be a bit tricky. Every country has its own rules for foreign nationals working within its borders.

Your new hire is going to need a visa. The United States is particularly dogged when it comes to work visas. The North American Free Trade Agreement (NAFTA) allows certain classes of professionals from Mexico and Canada to come to the United States to work with relatively little struggle. If you're planning on hiring from other countries, the visa process is likely to be cumbersome.

However, you do need to make sure the paperwork is in order, including an offer letter that includes specific elements. Should your prospective employee manage to secure a NAFTA TN visa, they will be allowed to remain in the country for three years. Unfortunately, the United States currently disallows TN visa family members to work. The TD visa, afforded to spouses and children of TN holders, is not work eligible.

There are other classes of visas that allow permanent stay and permit spouses to work. Those often require more intensive employer sponsorship, including a significant cash commitment. These are not available at all times during the year, and even if you qualify, you may not be selected for one.

If you plan on hiring talent from abroad to work in the United States, it's best to consult an immigration attorney for guidance. It can be traumatic for both the employee and the company to get too far into the hiring process only to find out that a visa issue (whether logistics or expense) sinks the deal.

If you're moving to hire someone from another country that you hope will stay indefinitely, you should have a long-term strategy. It might be tempting to use the easiest visa program, but that could set you up for trouble. This isn't an issue strictly limited to the United States (which has increasingly stringent visa requirements). Canadian companies should be aware of these issues, too.

"What we see happen often is that a company hires a worker with a limited duration work permit without much consideration of what will happen when the work permit expires," says lawyer Hilary Henley of McMillan. "Then, about two months before the work permit expires, they are looking for ways to extend it. Often, that is not possible. The result is that the worker gets sent back to their home country and the company loses the investment they have in that worker. However, with a long term plan in place, that worker could still come in on the limited duration work permit, but with a plan to apply for PR—permanent residency. PR applications take a long time to get together because the worker needs to get degree equivalency certificates, medical exams, and language testing—even if English is their first language. But those are things that the worker can start planning in order to make their application in advance of the expiry of their work permit."

Companies should consider hiring an attorney (or requiring employees to do so) to assist with immigration and work visa issues. Mistakes can cause significant delays that can severely impact employment eligibility.

"For the company's protection, any job offer made to foreign workers should always be conditional of the worker obtaining and maintaining legal status to work in Canada, but from a practical perspective, the company could be advising these new hires to get started on their permanent residency application and telling them about the timelines and the requirements," Henley says. "If the company wants to hire a lawyer to assist with the application, they can, but they can certainly just tell the worker that it is their responsibility to attend to their immigration status and advise them that time is of the essence with these applications. Shameless plug for hiring a lawyer—all immigration applications are lengthy and detailed, and any error or omission will result in denial and having to start over again so hiring someone who knows the system and the pitfalls can help prevent unnecessary denials that slow the process even further."

The UK is currently in flux due to Brexit proceedings, which could throw work visa regulations into upheaval. Currently, employers are required to obtain a sponsor license for any workers outside the European Economic Area and Switzerland.

Licenses are awarded for four years and range in price from £536 to £1,476. Costs depend on what kind of worker you seek to employ. The two options are skilled workers with long-term jobs (called "Tier

2") and skilled temporary workers (called "Tier 5"). You'll need a separate license for each tier.

The UK offers work visas to a wider array of professions than the United States, including public relations professionals and marketing executives, in addition to those directly involved in game development. As a sponsoring employer, you are required to ensure that those you hire have skills and credentials that satisfy the eligible position's responsibilities. Additionally, you must only sponsor those individuals filling roles that meet one of the eligible job types.

Failure to adequately monitor sponsored employees and maintain documentation supporting their credentials and job eligibility could result in the loss of license. It's a smart idea to employ a human resources professional prior to seeking authorization to sponsor employees, as failure to maintain accurate records could put all of your international workers at risk of expulsion from the country.

IN THIS CHAPTER,
WE LEARNED...

1. How to properly classify workers in the U.S., Canada, and the UK.
2. How to calculate the true cost of hiring.
3. What employers need to consider when hiring foreign workers.

CHAPTER FOUR

WHAT WILL A PUBLISHER PAY FOR?
(AND WHAT WON'T THEY COVER)

As your studio grows and your projects become more ambitious, you're likely going to have a decision to make. You can stay purely independent, bankroll your own games, and remain the captain of your own destiny.

Alternatively, you might have an idea that's too big for your bank account and revenue streams. In that case, the right publisher can help bring your game to market.

For the purposes of this chapter, we'll fast-forward through your prototype development and pitching. So, congratulations are in order! A publisher wants to sign your game. Let's talk about what to expect.

WHY DO I WANT TO WORK WITH A PUBLISHER (AND HOW DO I GET PAID)?

Chances are you went on the hunt for a publishing deal because you couldn't afford to make the game you wanted to. There's no shame in that. Big ideas require big financial support.

That funding won't all come up front, though. Disbursements will be made at agreed-upon points throughout the project, called **"milestones[1]."** This not only protects the publisher from studio financial mismanagement, it helps developers stay focused on efficiency and the negotiated timeline. Milestone structures are not standardized. They can be evenly split across a project or be variable throughout. They could also be based on up-front costs, alpha, beta and launch completion.

The safest thing for you to do as a developer is make sure that your milestones cover expenses. Cash flow is so very important. Leave enough timing buffer, so if a publisher rejects the terms of a milestone you have a month or two to fix. In short: look at your budget and your milestone payments, make sure there's never more money going out than the milestones brought in and you've got a couple months extra cash in case a milestone doesn't hit.

Your role in a publishing deal is to make your game. The publisher is responsible for enabling that (within the bounds of your contract), providing tools and services that might be challenging for you to tackle on your own, and making sure that people know about your game. That last point is a key step on the road to people actually purchasing your game.

This isn't free money. It's essentially an advance on your share of the revenue called a "recoup." As an example, if your publisher is providing $250,000 to make your game, you will owe that amount from your revenue share. Many publishers use the 100 percent recoup model, meaning the first $250,000 of your revenue share will be used to pay back the publisher for development costs.

Other recoup models exist, though most are reserved for established studios. You can read more about recoup models and calculations in Chapter 6 of *The GameDev Business Handbook*.

---

[1]   **Milestones** - An event marking a significant change in development.

WHAT WILL A PUBLISHER PAY FOR?

Every publisher handles contracts differently, though there are some common items your partner will likely handle. Other costs might go above and beyond the base funding level.

DEVELOPMENT

By the time you're negotiating a publishing agreement, you've settled on a budget for the project. Your milestone payments are intended to fund your work to create the game. This is why studios seek publishers.

PUBLIC AND PRESS RELATIONS

Your publisher should either have internal PR professionals, a contract with an outside agency, or both. It's often the publisher's responsibility to make contact with the media, secure coverage of your game, line up interviews, and distribute assets, preview code, and review copies.

MARKETING

It's a good idea to chat with your publisher about how your game will be marketed to consumers. Your partner might have a **boilerplate**[2] plan that gets tailored and tweaked for each game. This might include working with influencers, booth space at trade shows like PAX or PSX, and purchasing pre-roll ads on YouTube, Twitch, and other networks.

Depending on your publisher, broadcast television ads may or may not be included in the marketing plan. If your publisher is willing and able to incorporate them into the plan, their production and airtime purchase will be an additional cost. This will be added to your recoup amount.

TRAVEL AND LODGING

While your game might make it to trade shows as part of the publishing agreement, there's no guarantee you'll be coming with. It's not uncommon for developer airfare, lodging, and **per diem**[3] to be a post-recoup expense. In other words, those costs will be added to your recoup above and beyond your development costs.

---

[2] **Boilerplate** - Standardized text.
[3] **Per Diem** - A per-day amount of food and beverage expenses that an employer or publisher agrees to reimburse.

QA

It doesn't do anyone any good to release a buggy or broken game. There is a strong likelihood that your publisher either has internal quality assurance staff or contracts out with a third-party provider. Depending on the contract, your QA costs might be capped, with anything above the ceiling added to your recoup.

LOCALIZATION

If your game is available in English, you might want to offer subtitles in other languages. You can also opt for regional voiceover. Be sure to ask your publisher about their intentions. You may find that there are no plans to localize subtitles or voiceover. The option might be available as an add-on to your recoup, though. Additionally, you may need to pay a localization company to translate your store text so you can sell your game in additional territories.

FIRST-PARTY RELATIONS AND STOREFRONT LISTING

It's important to know which party is responsible for getting your games onto digital storefronts. You want to be clear up front who is going to handle submissions and sales page creation. This is a hidden cost, because these efforts can take an enormous amount of time. It's not uncommon for the publisher to tackle this, but if it falls to you, be sure you identify who will do the work and account for that time in the budget.

WHAT HAPPENS IF I NEED TO FIND MY OWN QA COMPANY?

Depending on your game's features, you'll need different quality assurance and testing services. "Most of the developers that we work with primarily come to us for our core testing services," says Sudarshan Ranganathan, head of gaming at Ixie Gaming.

For those developers incorporating multiplayer features, QA companies can provide load testing (throwing a large number of users at multiplayer servers to see if they can handle heavy traffic), as well as security and performance services. These are factors you'll want to consider early on in your process, according to Sudarshan.

"This gives QA enough time to deep dive and explore the game fully," he says. "This always results in a more stable end product and much more favorable end user experience."

Financial considerations might prevent you from engaging QA throughout your process. In those cases, make the most of your testing budget.

"I would recommend developers contract for resources once they have a stable prototype and then scale up when the project is closer to release," Sudarshan advises. "This will give QA ample time to churn out most of the bugs and have a stable end product that is ready for release. For startups or small scale developers, we recommend a short burst QA that involves one to two weeks of testing with a small team. This will help to weed out most of the obvious issues and have the game look more refined. The timeframe I suggest for this is about two to four weeks before the developer is showcasing their game at a conference, meeting investors or publishers, or before release. The costs here are minimal and the developer can feel more confident in their game and can warrant any additional QA if required."

Quality assurance can cost between $1,000 and $2,000 per round of testing, and developers should anticipate many of these per project. This is dependent on the game's complexity and the number of people involved in the testing.

"While QA can be optimized by minimizing the team size and having the same team work on multiple platforms, a larger team size comes into play especially when there is multiplayer scenarios involved,"

Sudarshan explains. "Also, when we have teams that test both staging and live builds, an additional effort goes into testing and may require more members."

QA is typically priced at a flat hourly rate. According to Sudarshan, QA in most major game titles accounts for 20 to 30 percent of the total budget.

Many small and mid-sized developers continue to outsource their QA efforts. Bringing those positions in-house leads to increased overhead and carrying costs (see Chapter 3). Internal quality assurance positions also require additional hardware purchase and maintenance that might be prohibitive (or the funds might be better used on other items).

"I have noticed that most of the small to mid-scale studios— developers and publishers both—do not have any form of internal QA," Sudarshan says. "This has been due to the rising costs of hardware especially with the introduction of video games on smartphones. With outsourced QA firms who have readily available hardware and operate at low costs, most of them see a huge cost reduction in the long run."

Developers don't often have multiple console test units (let alone two different models of PlayStation 4 and three different types of Xbox One) or countless models of smartphones and tablets. Purchasing and maintaining hardware for internal testing can be prohibitively expensive. Working with a firm that specializes in these services means you'll have access to testing on every piece of hardware on which your game might run without the hassle and cost of maintaining those devices internally.

Working with an external QA company mitigates financial risk, giving developers the ability to be more nimble. The job gets done, and often QA companies have systems in place for providing deliverables in a standardized format. These deliverables include:

- Bug reports
- Daily or weekly status updates
- Project metrics
- Test cases

Most of the documentation can be tailored to developer needs, as each game has its own feature set and needs. Using an external QA company provides access to expertise and customized set of deliverables while minimizing risk.

HOW DO I GET MY GAME LOCALIZED IN DIFFERENT LANGUAGES?

There are 1.5 billion people who speak English **around the world**[4], making it one of the most pervasive languages on our planet. And yet, that still only accounts for 20 percent of the world's population. If your game is only available in one language, you're leaving at least 80 percent of the population (and a wide swath of the market) in the cold.

Depending on your goals and resources, you might consider localizing your game by having the text and subtitles translated into different languages. Most commonly, games are translated into French, Italian, German, and Spanish (FIGS). However, with **1.2 billion people in China's now-friendlier video game market**[5], we're seeing a

[4] Dylan Lyons. "How many people speak English, and where is it spoken?" *Babbel.com.* https://www.babbel.com/en/magazine/how-many-people-speak-english-and-where-is-it-spoken. (accessed February 21, 2018.)
[5] James Lane. "The 10 most spoken languages in the world," *Babbel.com.* https://www.babbel.com/en/magazine/the-10-most-spoken-languages-in-the-world (accessed February 21, 2018.)

number of titles translated into Simplified Chinese.

The process for translating your game is best left to professionals, who understand how to navigate idioms and turns of phrase that require nuanced conversion. Companies like MoGi Group also take into consideration the moral, social, and historical issues of the target country.

Whatever you do, don't rely on Google Translate, or you might **set us up the bomb**[6]. The results will likely be wildly inaccurate, and you'll run the risk of offending your audience with a slipshod effort.

When you're considering having your game translated into other languages, there are a number of factors to consider. "It comes down to three core factors: wordcount, language combinations or number of languages an item needs to be localized into, and deadline," says MoGi Group head of global operations Zoi Vitsentzou. "Deadline is an important one because shorter deadlines have a whole lot of implications you need to factor in like team size, availability, and prioritization."

Pricing is typically handled based on the source text and factored per-word or per-character. This is dependent on the originating language, as each has its own translation needs.

Depending on your deadline needs, most companies can scale up the number of people working on your project. Expediting a project like this will cause costs to rise, so leave yourself enough time.

According to Vitsentzou, the average translator can tackle 2,000 to 2,500 words per eight-hour day. Proofreading is an essential piece of the process. Editors can work through 5,000 to 6,000 words in an eight-hour period.

Thankfully, translations can be streamlined by professional shops to help developers manage costs.

"The industry tools we use are designed to exclude tags or variables that need to remain constant, making the translation a little more straightforward and allowing us to offer a better rate by differentiating between unique words and repeated words and terms," Vitsentzou explains. "When I say 'new words' I'm referring to words that appear only once in a string structure and so need individual

6   Winkie, Luke. "25 years later, 'All Your Base Are Belong to Us' holds up" The Daily Dot.
      https://www.dailydot.com/unclick/all-your-base-are-belong-to-us-25th-anniversary/
      (accessed February 21, 2018.)

attention, as opposed to recurring strings that can be duplicated."

Costs can vary widely among localization companies, and many offer free quotes. Additionally, there are a number of services you may want to take advantage of, in addition to straight text translation.

In addition to localizing your script, many companies in this field will convert your user interface; translate your game manual, website, and print content; examine your graphics for anything that may be culturally insensitive; provide quality assurance testing for localized versions, and arrange for voice over to accompany text localization. All of these come at additional cost.

Because proper localization has a number of steps, you'll want to decide early if a simultaneous launch in multiple languages is feasible. If so, it's important to get started with a localization company early in the process.

"Careful planning and early notification can allow agencies to block schedule teams for specific projects," Vitsentzou says. "This is hugely important as there is a lot more to the process for a localization team than just translation, for example familiarizing themselves with the build, building a terminology list, determining and agreeing on main key phrases and terms, and a whole lot more before the actual translation process begins."

As with most aspects of game development, there are things you can do to make the localization process easier. Developers who aren't accustomed to the process tend to make similar missteps that can raise the cost and complicate the endeavor.

"Sometimes developers just don't know enough about the process," Vitsentzou explains. "This can lead to a number of things like: receiving files at the last minute, making deadlines difficult to keep to; translators not having access to the build; no guidelines being provided in terms of the graphical user interface, like character limits; no access to previously translated material which may contain important information about terminology or style; a lack of game testing to provide information about existing bugs and issues; even right down to developers not checking if a game actually supports different languages with specific requirements—Arabic, for example, is a big one because of its different text direction."

Most localization companies don't discuss their rates publicly. However, a **2011 AdWeek article written by Lingo24 founder Christian Arno**[7] gives us some insight.

Arno estimates that French, Italian, German, and Spanish localizations cost between $160 and $275 per 1,000 words. The same 1,000 words are slightly more expensive ($190 to $325) in Danish, Dutch, Finnish, Icelandic, Japanese, Korean, Norwegian and Swedish. Most firms will quote you a "per word" price.

Costs are similar for other languages that do not use Western Latin characters. If both the source and target languages are relatively uncommon, you may need to pay more. Finally, the location of the firm you're working with matters. They have overhead costs, too. Companies in more expensive areas may charge as much as $0.10 more per word.

Other services, like translating and preparing manuals and companion printed materials are priced differently. Those can range from $75 to $150 per hour.

And remember, localization quality assurance (commonly abbreviated as LQA is an additional cost,) may require hiring a second company on a per-hour basis to check the work of the first company. You should also think about the alphabet required for all the regions you plan to localize into. A font you're using may not be available or have an additional charge for Cyrillic or Asian markets, so take that into consideration from the start.

[7] Christian Arno. "Localization is more than a game," *AdWeek.com.* February 4, 2011.
      http://www.adweek.com/digital/localization-is-more-than-a-game/.
      (accessed February 21, 2018.)

IN THIS CHAPTER, WE LEARNED....

1.   How publishing contracts are structured.
2.   Why you might consider working with an external QA company.
3.   What you need to know about localizing your game.

CHAPTER
FIVE

HOW DO I PAY FOR MUSIC IN MY GAME?

A WORD OF WARNING BEFORE WE BEGIN...

Overall, much about game development business practice is still in its infancy. Due to the industry's age, the speed at which changes occur—along with numerous other completely debatable reasons—there is a lack of standardization across systems. The same can't be said when crossing paths with musicians and actors.

With nearly a hundred years of modern institutionalized practices each, we need to be very clear that what we are about to cover here is a surface level treatment to provide basic understanding. There are numerous aspects of the relationship between game developer and musician we won't be touching on.

To use *The Wizard of Oz* as an example, we're going to show you there's a man behind the curtain, but we aren't going to explain the biology of that man, the techniques used to weave the clothing he wears, nor how the geopolitics of Oz got us to this point.

We're going to talk basic business and budgeting, but we won't cover the incredibly complex legal aspects of music purchasing, licensing, streaming and the general "who owns what and when?" Whatever you do with music... know that it's going to require a lawyer.

Now, on with the show!

We've come a long way from the days of silent text adventures and BIOS beeps. Music has become an integral part of the video game experience.

Whether you're looking to give flair to dramatic scenes, amp up the adrenaline during combat, or cue the player during stealthy infiltration, music matters. Building out the soundtrack to accompany your gameplay masterpiece is a unique process.

The way you'll approach composers and contract them to write your hero's anthem is different than how you'll work with artists, coders, producers, and everyone else. In fact, your composer might be the only member of your project that negotiates revenue share as part of their compensation.

There are different ways you might pay a composer, each of which has different impact on your budget and long-term revenue realization. In most cases, composer contracts are written to provide ownership of the music to the studio. As you'll read, composers may be open to negotiating these rights in exchange for a reduced fee or soundtrack publishing rights.

HOW DO I FIND A COMPOSER FOR MY GAME?

Be smart about finding the composer to make your game sing. Your network is your best tool for finding the right match.

"If you just put an open call out, that's a mistake," says composer Dale North (*Pac-Man Pop, Ray's the Dead*). "For every composer that you see, there's 500,000 of them just around the corner waiting, looking for work... it's tough out there. You only have to do it once to learn how hard it is to make an open call."

Instead, North recommends listening to game soundtracks to find someone who specializes in the kind of tunes you want. You'll save yourself time sifting through a flood of responses to an open call.

"I know people that only do EDM-style music. I know people that specialize in retro so much so that you'd be crazy to hire anyone else because they've studied the intricacies," North explains. "There are

people that have little boards ripped open of game systems that you can MIDI up and access it. You would call this guy specifically for someone that can generate sound through old chip sets or whatever."

It's also important to consider the tools you'll be using. It's important to find someone who can deliver the music in a way that fits your time constraints and technical needs. When making inquiries of your network (and eventually the composers themselves), be sure to ask relevant questions.

North recommends inquiring about the following:

- Turnaround time
- Specific sound types (EDM, retro, full orchestra)
- Technical tool experience (FMOD, Wwise, etc.)

"Sometimes we even have scenarios where a famous, more expensive talent does the main theme for a project, and another composer does the rest of the score incorporating that theme," says Scarlet Moon Productions label manager Jayson Napolitano.

If you happen to be working with a big name composer for the main title theme or end title theme, you'll need someone to flesh out the rest of the music. That person will need to be comfortable using established themes, arranging established music, and recomposing for different moments.

For instance, Lionhead worked with Danny Elfman for *Fable*'s main theme. The rest of the music was composed by Russell Shaw. This scenario is no longer exclusively the domain of big budget titles, as composers work on a breadth of projects.

"Music is as specific as the design side," North says. "You want the exact person and not just some guy."

Some composers work with a manager or agent. Napolitano works with a dozen composers (including Dale North), playing matchmaker and agent. He helps developers find the right fit for each team and project. His approach considers a range of factors.

"I'm usually looking at the genre, sound, or mood the team is looking for, their timeline, and their budget," Napolitano says. Composers are creative individuals who can typically do many different sounds. Experience in the particular style the developer is looking for helps, but also budget. We work with talent who have worked on Final Fantasy... but also talent that works mostly in the indie and mobile space. So maybe the guy who worked on Final Fantasy is cost-prohibitive, whereas the other composer might be able to do a great job with half the budget. Regarding timeline, if we have two composers who are equally suited for a project, and one is tied up with other work, then we can recommend the one who's not."

MIDDLEWARE MATTERS

Middleware plays an important role in today's video game music, sound design and implementation landscape. (We briefly mentioned middleware in Chapter 2 as a budget consideration, and you can read more about a sample of popular solutions in Chapter 9.)

Contemporary music in games has moved beyond audio looping and has become more closely tied to player actions. This added complexity necessitates powerful software solutions and people who know how to use them.

"Creating great sounding music and sounds is only half the battle," says Somatone Interactive creative director Dale Crowley. "Hiring composers and sound designers who understand the technical aspects of audio implementation is critical to getting a polished final result."

Middleware also helps weave the multitude of available effects and audio tracks into a digestible, pleasing soundscape. Without it, games would be a chaotic mess of blaring sirens and screaming voices all competing for attention.

"Let's take the example of a complex real-time strategy battlefield where potentially hundreds of units are all moving, firing, and being destroyed," Crowley explains. "Even if each individual sound is of the highest quality, it will sound like a cacophony if prudent use of audio tools such as Elias, WWISE, FMOD, CRI or Fabric is not employed. These tools allow you to limit the number of simultaneous voices, focus on the most important ones—HDR Audio—and even mix the game in real-time while the game is running on the console, phone, or device. In film, designers create the sound, but there is a critical stage where all the music, sounds, and dialog are mixed together on a soundstage. These tools allow you to do a similar process in real-time as the game is playing."

Each of the middleware options has its own costs and licensing model. You can read more about Elias, Wwise, Fabric, and FMOD in Chapter 9.

THE PROS AND CONS OF PAYING FOR MUSIC BY THE MINUTE

Once under contract with a composer, you might find yourself paying per minute of music. Rates vary depending on the composer and the scale of your studio.

"It's hard to say what the industry standard is given the varying size of developers out there, but expect a professional composer to charge $750 to $1,500 per minute of finished music, depending on who it is and how in demand they are, the style of music needed—intricate orchestration and authentic chiptunes may take additional time to produce—and the amount of music you're requesting," Napolitano says.

With no industry standard rate, musicians can start negotiations around $1,000 per minute of music. For smaller studios, a generous composer might accept $1,000 per song. If your studio releases a couple successful titles and you grow into a "**triple-I**[1]" studio, you may find composers requesting closer to $2,000 per minute.

Often, this is payable under normal terms (**net 30**[2]), invoiced at agreed-upon points in the work. Composers typically sign over intellectual property rights, so it's up to the developer to use as much or as little music as they choose. However, be aware that your decision not to use a piece after it's been commissioned, completed, and approved has no bearing on your payment obligation. You still need to compensate your composer.

When making initial contact with a composer, there are two ways to figure out how much music you'll be paying for. The first is to use a formula provided by composers to determine how much you'll need. The other is more common. Many developers ask composers what they can do within the allotted music budget.

Consider providing the following information to the composer:

- Number of songs and stingers
- Approximate length per song (and whether any of them loop or need definitive endings)

---

[1] **Triple-I** - A class of game projects typically defined by a combination of factors, including larger budgets (greater than $1 million), larger teams (greater than 10 employees), and polish rivaling titles released by mega-publishers. The term is derived from AAA (pronounced triple-A), denoting the biggest blockbusters in the video game industry, and typically implies top quality titles made without publisher funding.
[2] **Net 30** - Shorthand meaning due within 30 days of receipt.

- Genre or style
- Delivery format
- Any special implementation or engine considerations

You might provide this information to your composer in a streamlined format. Scarlet Moon Productions has created one for this purpose (available in this book's digital supplements).

There is a competing theory in the music world that by-the-minute payment structures are counterintuitive. The idea behind the opposing approach is that a soundtrack is more than the sum total of its length.

"I don't like the idea that the only way I can be of value is through writing music," says BAFTA Award winning composer Austin Wintory (*Journey, Assassin's Creed Syndicate*). "My favorite example, even though it's not a game, is the movie *Cast Away*, because *Cast Away's* a two-hour movie that has 14 minutes of score. And the 14 minutes of score is entirely localized to the last 20 minutes of the film. It's a creative decision. He gets off the island. The first time we ever hear a cue in that entire movie is when he clears the breakwaters with his homemade raft and sees what the island looks like from this objective outside perspective, and the first time he has distance from the island and sees what his home/prison for the last four years has looked like, and a simple string chord on an A-flat major comes in.

"I think it's a stroke of genius. I think it's one of the best scores I've ever heard in my life. And it's baby simple. And it literally uses only strings and a single oboe. And then they add piano for the end credits. We're talking 14 minutes of music total. And Alan Silvestri's rate in the late '90s was probably somewhere close to a million dollars; I would guess, $700,000, $800,000, $900,000 to do a movie, especially a big, high-profile Tom Hanks / Robert Zemeckis movie.

"And the idea that his contribution would be worth substantially less because they came to the creative revelation, the genius choice to put that little music in the film is insulting, because to me, music is made meaningful by the silence on either side of the musical experience in the same way that light is only meaningful against a backdrop of darkness. And so to say that when and where there should be silence is not part of the creative decision is ridiculous. And to take that out of the composer conversation is to say your only incentive is to write as much music as you possibly can and to jam it into every nook and cranny of the game."

Wintory's take on payment structures, especially through the lens of the *Cast Away* example, reminds us that composers who work in video games are developers, just like coders, artists, and writers. And from the perspective of composer-as-developer, Wintory suggests that the per-minute fee structure incentivizes composers to fill too much of the soundscape with music.

"I think games are over-scored. I think that games could benefit from breathing more," he says. "I think we should be in a constant dance between music and sound design. And I think the creative process of deciding when and how to do that is actually what you're paying for when you hire me. Yes, of course, I'm gonna try to write music that you like on its own terms. But the goal is to deliver a game, not an album, not a stack of tunes. And when you're delivering a game, when you are a game developer who focuses on music as their discipline within the world of game development, your job is to think of as a sum total package. So where and when music should go is part of that decision-making process. I can't stand the idea that saying, 'You know what would be really cool? What if there's no music here?' will take money out of your pocket to improve their game."

UNDERSTANDING THE "PACKAGE DEAL"

Many developers are moving away for the per-minute payment structure in favor of a fee-based approach to the process. At the same time, studios are expanding what it means to be a video game composer.

It used to be that composers were responsible for creating the score and handing it off to the studio. At that point, someone contracted by the developer would arrange for any necessary live orchestration and recording work.

Today, composers are increasingly responsible for delivering a complete score. The budgeting and negotiation process is no longer just about what it takes to write the music. Composers and developers both need to understand and incorporate the costs of live musicians, recording studios, equipment, and more.

"If we're hiring an orchestra, the costs associated with recording an orchestra score are many, and varied," Wintory explains. "There's a lot of detail, because it's not just, 'Let's get a room full of musicians and some microphones and off we go.' You have to know how to contract that orchestra to begin with. You have to understand that not everyone in the orchestra gets paid the same. If you have a 50-piece orchestra, which is a medium-sized group, you have to work with the contractor to figure out how your pay scales work. The concertmaster almost always makes double what everyone else is making. Your principal cello might be making one and a half. And then you have other things to consider. Do you have a large percussion section? Because there's almost always what they call cartage, or what they call in the UK porterage, which is a fee associated with transporting a truckload of big instruments like tympani and bass drums and all that to the studio. So you have to work out all that to even know what your musician costs are. Then you start getting into things like a librarian to handle all the sheet music and make sure everything's accounted for in the right order."

When you're looking at a package deal, you need to consider the following:

- The cost for composing the score
- Contracting the various musicians (soloists vs orchestra), with or without an intermediary contractor
- Coordinating studio time with personnel schedule and possible gear rental
- A librarian, who keeps track of the different parts
- A copyist, who is responsible for making sure all musicians have the music they need. This role might be combined with the librarian position, or not. If not, separate dedicated librarian position is required (most common when copying is done in different city from the recording)
- A studio engineer handling the recording and managing the assistant engineer
- A digital recordist, doing real-time take **comping**[3], file management, and more
- Miscellaneous other things such as transportation, food, and overtime

The debate over package deals is lively. Some composers feel it drives wages down. Others relish the opportunity to control all the details.

---

[3] **Comping** - The process of combining the best parts of multiple takes and piecing them together to create a seamless, better-sounding whole

Wintory explains the difference by recounting the tales of working on *Journey*, which wasn't a package deal, and Giant Squid's *Abzu*, which was.

"On *Abzu*, I didn't want a score with a normal orchestral sound," he says. "I wanted a very lean body of winds and strings. But then I also wanted to have a nice, lush choir, but a top-heavy choir. There were virtually no men. It was almost all women. And I wanted seven harps. If I had to run this all through a music department, they'd say, 'Could you do it with six harps?' and I'd end up getting back and forth. Look, let me just do it, OK? *Journey* was not a package deal. I had to do everything through Sony. And there were a few times I pitched crazy ideas, and they pushed back against me and they were very smart to do so. They dramatically improved my work, because they were this voice of reason. But in a case like *Abzu*, it would've been a little trickier or at least tedious, to have to greenlight every decision. I loved having the freedom, and Giant Squid, the developer, was basically like, 'Hey, man, do your thing. That's why we want you here.' So for me, the package deal was very appealing in that situation."

From the studio's perspective, package deals make things easier. The composer is handling everything related to the score and recording, delivering you a complete soundtrack when all is said and done.

However, you still need to have an understanding of reasonable costs. Whether you're paying them directly or building it into the composer's fee, you need to know how much musicians, engineers, editing, mixing, and mastering cost.

Composer and sound designer Kole Hicks breaks down his experience with these different expense categories in an article for **Designing Music Now**[4]. While geography, experience, and personal factors impact costs, Hicks offers some ballpark figures that can help orient budgeters. He estimates live musician costs at $100 or more per hour, depending on skill and position (remember, not every musician is paid equally).

Studio space can start at $50 an hour for small rooms that can only hold a soloist or a few musicians. That scales upward as spaces get larger and equipment needs expand, reaching $300 per hour or more. Large rooms that can hold a full orchestra will likely cost even more, so call around in your area to get a sense of pricing in your market.

---

[4]   Kole Hicks. "Budgeting for Audio in Your Game's Crowdfunding Campaign," *Designing Music Now*. May 16, 2016. https://www.designingmusicnow.com/2016/05/16/budgeting-audio-crowdfunding-campaign/. (accessed February 26, 2018).

Your recording engineer will likely range between $50 and $150 per hour, depending on skill and geography. You may need to hire an editor, also. That typically costs at least $50 per hour.

MAKING THE MOST OF YOUR SOUNDTRACK

The market for video game music is growing, and fans are hungry. You may not have any plans to sell your soundtrack, but your composer might want to take on that responsibility. It's not uncommon for a developer to offer distribution rights to the composer.

In those cases, unless you bundle your soundtrack with your game on Steam and other digital distribution platforms, you won't have to deal with the music revenue. All of those funds would, instead, go directly to the composer (who will be doing the heavy lifting to distribute on Bandcamp, Steam, and other platforms).

"It benefits the composer to allow bundling, so you can come to an agreement about who keeps what share of that sale," Napolitano advises. "If the game was crowdfunded, you might address how the music is distributed to backers of that Kickstarter campaign. You might include in the contract who's responsible for creating visual assets for the soundtrack release. You might also consider requirements about promotion in terms of what the composer can't discuss in interviews and whether there's any obligation on either side to promote the composer, the music, or soundtrack release."

If you already have a process in place for publishing and selling soundtracks, there's still a way to collaborate with the composer. You may, for instance, only want to cover major distribution channels, like iTunes and Amazon. Your composer might want to publish the game elsewhere.

"I love having Bandcamp as a platform for my soundtrack albums," Wintory says. "Unsurprisingly, because Assassin's Creed is such a big franchise and Ubisoft is such a big publisher, they said, 'We're going to own this for sure.' Our deal is built from a foundation of a work for hire, so I asked them, 'I know that you've probably never done this, but can we co-publish the soundtrack album?' There ended up being multiple record labels involved because there's Ubisoft's own record label for digital distribution, UBILOUD. And that's how they sell the soundtrack on iTunes. Then they also licensed the rights to make physical CDs to Sumthing Else Music. And they also licensed the rights to me and my record label, which I call T-65b records to be able to co-publish it on Bandcamp."

WHAT HAPPENS WHEN YOU WANT GREAT MUSIC, BUT HAVE A SMALLER BUDGET?

There are a number of ways to save a bit of money when working with a composer that are equitable to both parties. When you're commissioning music, most of the time, developers have an expectation that they will outright own the compositions. You're paying a premium to own the music.

There are other ways to handle payment, ownership, and licensing that might help you get the sound you're looking within your budget. However, most attorneys and studios approach the process as an all-or-nothing proposition.

"One of the challenges of the game industry is that it's still carrying the baggage of the software industry," Wintory says. "A lot of its legal infrastructure is built around that corporate intellectual property mentality that says billion-dollar companies can rise and fall based on a single line of code. That means that anything any employee makes has the potential to completely make or break that company. So it non-negotiably must be that all employees, everything they make is owned by that company, too."

(You can read more about invention assignment clauses and working on passion projects in Chapter 3 of The GameDev Business Handbook.)

There's an inherent fear that licensed music can cause problems down the road. If licenses expire, then a developer has a hard decision to make about whether to renew the contract, pull the game from sale, or make changes to the music. However, composers can work with developers to make sure that both parties are protected.

You can build a number of protections into the contract that allow for composer ownership while ensuring you never have to pull your game from sale for music-related reasons, including:

- An indefinite and irrevocable license
- A provision that allows music to be used without reservation for marketing and promotion
- A clause that allows the music to be used at no additional charge for sequels and spin-off projects

"On games like *The Banner Saga*, for example, I completely and totally own everything outright," Wintory explains. "The contract language on a game like that is that *The Banner Saga* developer, Stoic Studio, is licensing the music from me, which on paper is indistinguishable as if I had written it beforehand and they were just licensing existing music."

Another option is to defer a portion of your payment until after your game ships. When working with employees, you'll be compensating them on an established payroll cycle (bi-weekly, semi-monthly, or monthly, usually). Contractors typically get paid 30 days after they invoice for their work. Neither of these groups often receives revenue share (a percentage of post-release net income).

Composers sometimes work differently. A small (but significant enough) amount of time, composers will forego some or all up-front revenue in exchange for a percentage of revenue. This is often called "points on the back-end" or revenue share.

If you can't afford to pay your contractor their rate up front, you can offer a revenue share agreement. There's no guarantee your offer will be accepted, but there is no harm in trying.

WHEN IS UNUSED WORK "WASTED" (AND WHEN ISN'T IT)?

Unused work is a killer across the development process. This holds true with regard to the soundtrack, as both parties stand to lose quite a bit when unused work becomes waste.

Remember, composers may charge by minute of music. Whether they spend two hours or two days on one minute, they are still receiving the same fee. It's important to provide your composer enough information up front so you get what you want.

In addition to the number of minutes and number of songs you'll need, you should consider the genre and feel. Since many composers are brought in late in the project, art, gameplay, and other assets can assist in creating the perfect soundtrack for your game.

The more detail you provide up front, the more likely you'll get what you want on the first or second pass. Many composer contracts include a revision clause that limits how many passes are required under the base fee. Most of these limit developers to two revisions, but open communication can help create flexibility. If handled poorly, requesting too many revisions due to indecision or poor direction can burn bridges.

"Sometimes when I vent after a long 10-hour day of just trying to make a revision work, the thing that I always end up saying is I just flushed money down the toilet today. Just continually grabbed fistfuls of cash and flushed it," North explains. "On the flip side, when things go well, it feels like you're printing money. It's like if music comes from you organically and you're just in perfect sync with your client and they're saying, 'You have this sound and it's exactly what we want and we trust you,' and you make a song and you deliver it and they pay you your rate, that's like magic."

There is a counter perspective on the "wasted work" phenomenon. Sometimes it's possible to repurpose music during the process.

"I'm a believer that if I write a **cue**[5] and then I discover it's not working, that discovery was worth writing the cue for," Wintory states. "It's almost a logical impossibility to truly waste work. The only situation where that's semi-true is if like they cut a whole level from a game and all the music that we wrote for it went with it. But even that's not necessarily wasted, because you learn about the aesthetic of the game in that process, and sometimes they'll say, 'Oh, we really liked that cool thing you did in that one sequence of the level, and we think that there's a way to use that elsewhere even though it's not going to be exactly the same.'"

---

[5] **Cue** - A piece of music used in television, film, or video games.

89

When Wintory worked on thatgamecompany's *Journey*, he ran into a situation that allowed him to use music from a cut segment in another area. While this isn't the norm, it's a good idea for both developers and composers to look for these opportunities.

"In the opening part of the game is an open desert. In the very early stages, when we were still trying to figure out what the point of that whole section was going to be, there was a prototype of a nasty sandstorm. You had to hide to avoid it blowing you all the way back to the beginning of the level. It always looked like ass and it wasn't fun. It didn't say anything meaningful. It just seemed like everyone thought, 'Oh, well, it's a desert. Let's put a sandstorm in.' Of course, that whole thing got cut. But then later in the game, they implemented a storm system in the mountain. I had done my due diligence on violent music in the context of a game that's otherwise extremely, obsessively nonviolent. I'd already figured out what the aesthetic for that can be, and so I already had a head start to figure out how to handle the snowstorms because of this completely cut feature earlier."

Sometimes unused work is an inevitability that can lead to a better final product. Working with composers early in the process can create a score that's more tightly integrated into design. This is more time-intensive, but involving soundtrack considerations before too much is solidified can lead to a more cohesive package.

"There's some value in having a composer working on your project early on," Napolitano explains. "They can often produce something relatively quickly that encapsulates the themes or moods you're aiming for, and the rest of the team can listen to what they create while they're working on the rest of the game's assets. That's fine if they're working on a revenue share basis, or focusing solely on your project, but in instances where you're paying per minute or per track, it might be cost-prohibitive to have music created that may not fit the needs of the final product. For that reason, music is often brought on towards the end of production when gameplay, story, and visuals are already completed. This allows the composer to score what's there or have a final view of what players will be experiencing in the cases of looping music."

From the composer's perspective, coming onto the project earlier can be a coveted opportunity. There's better integration with the creative process when music is part of the early design process.

"I'm doing a game now, and my manager was able to open the developer's mind to the idea of us doing this together along the way," North explains. "It might be a little weird and different from just ordering music like you're used to, but there's a lot of cool things we can do if we do that. Since then, we've been able to bring in noted Japanese vocalists and do some really cool things where music cross-fades. Because the game is so early in development, we are able to shape very specifically how that was going to look and feel."

While both methods work, you're likely to get something completely different from the composer if you start early. North says that composers really don't need much information about your game to get started, and they can also come in close to the end of the process. If you start early, the composer will be more invested in your vision.

"If you wait until the very end, you're just very quickly conveying to me what you need from a music standpoint in terms of feel and genre," he says. "If I'm working with you from the beginning and seeing assets as they come out I'll be talking to you about designs of this monster level or pacing. I'm going to know through my own experience and creative process what that sounds like, versus being at the very end and you giving me a link of some YouTube video that had a cool song that you liked. It's so different. It feels like I work in game development versus being a hired gun to just finish out this thing."

Both North and Wintory say there is value in being involved early. "That's such a favored position and place to be in that I don't think any composer would want to discourage anyone they're working with from considering it," North says.

"I love to be as early as possible. I love to have as much time as possible because I love to explore," Wintory adds. "I love having opportunities to try things that will fail and to kick over rocks that lead to dead ends. And if we don't have that kind of time, then you have to be a little safer in your choices, and that's never my preference. But the good news is, fortunately, in the game industry, they almost always come to you earlier than is needed to do the work. I mean,

I've almost never, only on a few games have I ever felt like the clock was ticking to an extreme, because I've done quite a lot of movies, and movies you almost always have like four or five weeks. It's just standard. And I've only once or twice had that kind of timeframe on games. It's almost always been at least several months, if not several years."

It's important to note that coming into a project early is relative. For smaller, linear games, that could be during the concepting or pre-production phases. Open-world games take longer to get underway, because the foundational work is so much heavier.

"For *Assassin's Creed Syndicate*, they'd already been working on the game for several years, but it was largely technical work." Wintory says. "They still were very much figuring out the storyline, because a game like that has such high startup costs of building out the world. In the case of *Syndicate*, it was building out Victorian London. You spend a year just creating the map, so there's not much for a composer to do at that point. You can sit there and play around with themes and aesthetics all you like, but sometimes even the writers don't quite know what it's going to be yet. They're still in their brainstorming mode. So there's no way to even know if your ideas are right. In that case, even though they've been on it for several years, I probably was brought in at the right time, which was about a year from it finishing."

BEWARE COMMON MISTAKES

Scarlet Moon Productions label manager Jayson Napolitano manages a dozen composers and a large number of relationships with developers. He's seen contracts go right… and go wrong.

With years in the industry under his belt, Napolitano offers advice and a cautionary tale for developers and composers.

Music is a big part of any game, and cutting corners can diminish the impact of the final product immensely. So sometimes working with a friend, while cheap and fun, can be a detriment to the project if they're not up to the task.

That being said, I'd say a big mistake developers make with composers is pigeonholing them. I'm always greatly appreciative when a client works with us on a game, then comes back to us to work on a completely different game type requiring a completely different sound. That developer recognizes that composers are creative individuals that are a capable of producing a variety of different sounds.

The most important thing when working with a composer is their compatibility with you and your team and their work ethic. There are countless proficient composers out there, many of whom can deliver what you need, so once you have a pool of competent talent to consider—and trust me, you won't have to search, as they'll come to you—work to assess those two things.

Ask if it's OK to speak with some of their previous clients to make sure they were communicative and delivered on time. Things will always come up, but you really want a composer who will communicate with you regularly and do their best by you. You have to take care of each other in this business, because things rarely go as planned, so find a composer who you're confident will do that.

The other mistake is giving a composer mixed signals as it relates to your needs. We've had clients tell us they want to give us creative freedom to do what we want, then have an endless list of revision requests when we do that. You really need to decide what it is you want. We use this sound document (included in this book's digital supplements) that anyone can feel free to use that captures all of your thoughts. Any composer will appreciate you having filled this out as it will give them guidance for how the assets should sound.

We require this from every client. Sometimes it's filled out very thoroughly with tons of reference tracks, other times it's a little lighter, which suggests some degree of creative freedom. Everyone needs to be on the same page before work commences, though, to prevent revisions and delivery delays.

I've been fairly lucky in avoiding some of the worst pitfalls of this business. However, we were working with a composer who had a slate of projects that they needed to deliver on. We stepped in to negotiate rates and delivery timelines where they hadn't existed before.

This artist was grappling with some life situations that prevented them from delivering music on time. I did keep the clients up to date, and did get extensions as needed, but after months of not being able to move forward, several of those clients had to move on to find another solution.

This lesson reiterates the need for constant communication, the setting up of delivery milestones, and for ongoing assessment to make sure things are on track. It's up to the developer to take a firm stand, assess the situation on a case-by-case basis—again, life happens on both sides, and some delays should always be expected—and move on if need be.

CLANGS AND BANGS: BUILDING OUT THE REST OF YOUR SOUND DESIGN

While you can certainly license pre-recorded sound effects at **$1 to $5 per effect**[6], you may want someone to create sounds specifically for your game. According to Hicks, the cost per audio effect can vary dramatically depending on the experience and skill level of your sound designer. Costs can start as low as $20 per effect, but climb to more than $100 per effect when working with an industry veteran.

The nature of the effect also has an impact on cost. Simple effects, like footsteps, can be significantly less expensive. However, if your project requires **field recording**[7], the costs can be significantly higher per effect.

You might have need for a large number of effects, in which case daily or project-based fees (rather than per-effect fees) might be preferable for your budget and the sound designer. Median daily rates are typically $300 to $400, with sound designer skill and geography nudging those expenses higher or lower.

You might be able to save money on a tight budget by negotiating ownership of the created effects. That can reduce costs by as much as half. If you and your designer agree on this approach, it's a good idea to ensure the contract gives you indefinite and irrevocable license to use those effects for your game and any other titles in the IP.

---

[6] "Sound Effects Downloads," SoundRangers.
    http://www.soundrangers.com/index.cfm/category/1/sound-effects.
    cfm??CFID=47d3d5ce-8dd1-4440-a811-763aa55fb1a6&CFTOKEN=0.
    (accessed February 27, 2018).
[7] **Field recording** - Audio recorded outside the studio, like gunshots or animal sounds.

WHAT IF I WANT TO USE POPULAR MUSIC?

Perhaps you don't want to commission new music for your game. This is especially common if you're making a rhythm game that relies on familiar music.

Be prepared to enter a tangled web of rights, licenses, and performance royalty organizations (PROs). The music licensing world is complex, with organizations and practices dating back to the days of the player piano. An **outstanding explainer**[8] written by *The Verge's* Sarah Jeong can give you just a taste of what you're in for.

If you still decide to dive into music licensing, you'll need to negotiate on a song-by-song basis. There is no studio better versed in this topic than Harmonix. With thousands of songs across Rock Band, Dance Central, and *DropMix*, studio personnel have made themselves the foremost experts on working popular music into video games.

"Most people don't know that there are two sides to every song—the audio recording and the creative work. In basic terms, the audio recording or 'master' is the music that you hear," explains Harmonix head of music strategy and partnerships Cheryl Gehbauer. "The creative work, known as the 'composition', is everything that goes into the creation of the song—from the notes and lyrics you see if

[8] Sarah Jeong. "A $1.6 billion Spotify lawsuit is based on a law made for player pianos," *The Verge.* March 14, 2018. https://www.theverge.com/2018/3/14/17117160/spotify-mechanical-license-copyright-wixen-explainer. (accessed March 15, 2018).

the work is put down on paper by the songwriters, to the producers' contributions. The creators of the music composition might not be the artists on the master recording."

It's not always as simple as contacting only the songwriter and the performer. There can be a number of rights holders if the song is co-written, the producer has ownership, or if multiple performers contributed to the recording. Things can be further complicated as rights might cover worldwide use or be restricted to specific territories.

"You must be sure to have 100 percent approval to use the master and 100 percent approval to use the composition for the territories in which you intend to release your game," Gehbauer says. "You are responsible for contacting and securing approval from all of the required master rights holders as well as all of composition rights holders. In general, for popular recorded music, record labels control the master rights and music publishers control the composition rights."

A search online will usually turn up which label released a song. Publishing details are a bit trickier. You'll want to become familiar with both the American Society of Composers, Authors, and Publishers (ASCAP) and Broadcast Music, Inc. (BMI). These are the PROs we mentioned earlier.

PROs are a clearinghouse for performance royalty payments, and they have a long, pervasive reach. If you've ever worked for a radio station, performing arts organization, or a restaurant that plays music, you've probably had a relationship with ASCAP or BMI (even if you didn't know you should have been paying them).

Once you have that information, prepare your license terms. You'll need to send the same terms to everyone involved in both sides of the song.

In order to determine what those terms are, you'll need to start with the music budget. To put shape to this piece of your financial puzzle, Gehbauer recommends asking yourself the following questions:

- How many songs do you need? Will you license songs individually or try to engage in blanket deals?
- How are you planning to use the music?

- How much of the song do you need? Will you use a few seconds or do you need the full length of the song?
- How long would you like to sell the game? This is the term for which you need to license the music.
- In what territories are you releasing the game during that term? Your needs today, might not be the same next year or later in the term.
- There is a ton of music in the world to be licensed. Do you need popular music to sell your game? Can you get creative with developing artists?

"If you need hundreds or thousands of songs, you may want to contact record labels and music publishers to engage in blanket license deals, which could give you access to their shares of a large number of songs," Gehbauer advises. "You still need to be sure that you clear 100 percent of both sides of each song for territories, if you engage in blanket deals. Each rights holder can only approve their share of a song, even under a blanket deal."

Costs and payment structures vary depending on your needs and the rights holders. **According to ASCAP**[9], there are sales-based compensation structures and full buyouts. These can range from $0.08 to $0.15 per composition in a sales-based model. Buyouts, which are a flat fees independent of sales volume, can range from $2,500 to more than $20,000 per composition.

Additionally, you should think ahead to whether you'd like to sell your game's soundtrack. If so, this will be an additional negotiation item and will likely require a separate royalty.

"In any case, you should consult a music attorney, who can ensure you are requesting all the rights and securing all the licenses needed in order to release your game," Gehbauer recommends.

If you want to use licensed music, you'll need to leave yourself enough time to complete the process. You'll need to find all the rights holders, negotiate terms, and wait for approvals. Gehbauer recommends allotting at least six months for the process. If you need to license a large volume of compositions, the process could take even longer.

[9] Todd Brabec and Jeff Brabec. "Licensing Songs for Video Games," ASCAP. 2007. https://www.ascap.com/Home/Music-Career/articles-advice/ascapcorner/corner16.aspx. (accessed March 15, 2018).

"Keep in mind this is a negotiation," Gehbauer says. "All of these terms are levers than can be pulled to work within your budget. Open a discussion with the labels and publishers to find a solution that works for everyone. There is music for every budget."

Unless you negotiate an indefinite term, at some point music licensing is going to present a challenge for continued sales of your game. As time starts to tick down toward the expiration date, you might want to renew the agreement.

"Be sure to leave enough time to research all the rights holders involved and make your case," Gehbauer says. Rights holders change pretty frequently. You will need to research all the current rights holders and seek their approval."

If you decide not to re-license music or can't come to terms, you'll need to remove your game from sale. It's often a good idea to give potential customers notice, as this can spur purchases from those that might not want to play your game right now, but want to leave themselves the option to do so later. For physical copies, you'll likely have a limited amount of time after the license expiration to sell off remaining inventory.

The other option in this case is to remove and replace the music you're no longer authorized to use with new, more cost-effective tunes. This is easier to execute on PC storefronts. For console versions, expect to go through a certification pass. If you don't leave yourself enough time to make these changes, you might have no choice but to remove your game from sale for a period of time.

IN THIS CHAPTER,
WE LEARNED...

1. How to find the right composer for your game.
2. A method for estimating music costs.
3. How to make a smart decision about licensed versus original music.

CHAPTER
SIX

WHAT SHOULD I EXPECT WHEN HIRING SOMEONE TO WRITE MY GAME'S STORY?

In the beginning, there were only words. OK, maybe text adventures weren't the absolute beginning of the video game revolution, but they were a crucial step on our path to today's big-budget, graphically gorgeous behemoths.

You may have a general idea for your game's story, but might find yourself stumped when you try to put the script together. Don't worry. That's completely normal.

There's a writer out there that can spin the straw of your great concepts into narrative gold. Finding the right person for the job will mean tapping into your network and doing your research.

THE PERFECT WRITER OR NARRATIVE DESIGNER FOR YOUR PROJECT IS OUT THERE

You don't need to settle for any ol' writer. It's important to find someone who has the skills to write for games. Not every wordsmith can work in this medium.

"I recommend finding game narratives you like, then reaching out to whoever is listed as writer and/or narrative designer. It seems simplistic, but it works," says writer Walt Williams (*Spec Ops: The Line, Star Wars Battlefront II*). "Game writing and narrative design is an acquired skill, because to do both well, you need an understanding of how design and production work, plus the appropriate expectations of where story stands in the development hierarchy. Pulling in a great writer from another medium may seem like a good idea, but if they don't know what they're in for, it probably won't be a fruitful relationship."

There are resources available you can use to start becoming familiar with writers and the craft. The International Game Developers Association (IGDA) maintains a **writing special interest group (SIG)**[1]. The website includes blog posts on writing and forums to discuss issues in the field. Additionally, the annual Game Developers Conference (GDC) offers a narrative summit.

Before you start your search for a scribe, you'll need to examine what you want from the relationship. Williams suggests considering the following elements before reaching out to potential partners:

- Scope of work – Some writers are brought on to write the **critical path**[2] (main story). That could be a linear affair or involve branching dialog and story development. Other writers handle generic and **systemic content**[3]. You'll need to know approximately how long the game will be and an estimated line count (with distinction between the main script and systemic lines)

- Engine work – Will the narrative designer need to work with your engine, or are they just responsible for the words?

---

[1] "SIGs: Game Writing," IGDA.org. http://www.igda.org/group/game-writing. (accessed February 8, 2018).
[2] **Critical path** - The shortest path through a game, typically comprised of content only pertaining to the main story.
[3] **Systemic dialog** - Lines non-player characters shout in response to player actions. Also called "barks."

- Development progress – How far along is the game? Is the story mostly nailed down, or will the writer have more creative freedom?

- Delivery timing – How soon do you need the script?

- Tone check – You might not want to hire a comedy writer to pen your blood-soaked horror game. Understanding what kind of feel you want from the story and dialog is important for finding the right person to craft your narrative. Make sure you have a good idea of what tone you want from your game before you start talking to writers. "I once had a developer tell me they wanted the game to be funny, and then referenced a death scene from *Aliens*. It was nonsense," Williams recalls. "If a developer can't correctly interpret the tone of a film or TV show, they definitely won't do it in their own game, and you'll be in for a long, hard slog. Good to know that up front."

There are wrong ways to make an approach. Remember that writers are creative professionals and not automata.

"Avoid the story robot approach," says Rhianna Pratchett (*Tomb Raider, Rise of the Tomb Raider*). "It's the quite austere, 'We are looking for a writer to generate a thousand lines of dialogue. Can you give us your rate?' type of thing. They're just looking for the numbers associated with it. They've decided it's going to be X number of lines, and they'd like to find out how much they're going to have to pay for X number of lines. That's what they're going to post into the story robot, and hopefully the words will come out."

WHAT ARE THE WAYS I CAN WORK WITH A WRITER?

There are two primary ways to work with a writer on your game. They can either be a lead or an asset creator. Williams draws the distinction in terms of stakeholders.

"A project lead is the main narrative stakeholder," Williams says. "They work with the other leads to craft a narrative that best serves the project. They ensure art and design support that narrative through regular review, feedback, and working one-on-one with the other disciplines. They also write the script – or at the least, oversee a team of writers."

Writers can also be tasked with "asset creation." In this case, the writer is preparing dialog and incidental lines within the scope of someone else's narrative vision. Within that broad label are a number of different roles:

- Dialog
- Cinematics
- Barks (incidental/systemic dialog)

"On *Rise of the Tomb Raider*, I worked a lot on the cinematics, and some other secondary narratives," Pratchett explains. "They had another writer that was doing level dialog, and another that was doing documents, and then another that was helping polish."

Bringing an additional writer closer to the end of development doesn't necessarily mean your project is in trouble. When everything is going well, that person is simply a fresh pair of eyes that can help clean and polish before launch.

"Phillip Gelatt, who was our fresh pair of eyes on *Rise of the Tomb Raider*, he slotted in very well," Pratchett says. "He knew that his role was to enhance and support what we had already done. His job wasn't to rewrite everything, but to try and support the vision that had already been established and just be honest, but also diplomatic as well. And he was very good at that."

The other occasion for bringing a writer on late in the project is for emergency script repair. Sometimes your initial writer doesn't work out or needs assistance to bring the story across the finish line.

"I've talked about being contacted very late in a project. That's what I call being a narrative paramedic," Pratchett explains. "Avoid situations where you end up looking for a narrative paramedic. So your story is dying and you are desperate for someone to come in and save it. And it's usually dying because you haven't had writers or designers in the mix. Or maybe you have, and they haven't worked out... certainly that happened a lot when the industry got very obsessed with Hollywood writers. That's still there to a certain degree. And often the Hollywood writers didn't really know what they were writing for, and the developers didn't really know how to talk to the writers. And so what you would end up with might be an interesting script for a movie, but didn't really work for a game, because those strong communication loops weren't in place. That used to generate a lot of work for game writers having to narrative paramedic those kind of scripts."

That's not to say that you shouldn't seek emergency writing help if you need it. It's more about approaching writers transparently so they know what to expect.

"If it is a narrative paramedic gig, be honest and be direct about it," Pratchett advises. "Don't kind of dance around it. There's obviously writers that will take those kind of gigs, that see that as a challenge. You want to try and engage a writer as early on as possible."

Once you start working with larger budgets, you might decide to work with a writing team. *Tomb Raider* (2013) had two writers (Pratchett and John Stafford). That expanded to four people for the sequel, *Rise of the Tomb Raider.*

"Even then, with AAA games, that's a fairly small to average writing team size these days," explains Pratchett. "And when you're talking about the AAA echelons, like teams for Ubisoft's games, or *The Witcher*, or things like that... they're massive compared to us."

This isn't to say that a single writer can't carry a full game from start to finish. Pratchett tackled both Triumph Studios' *Overlord* and *Overlord II* as a solo writer.

She also urges developers not to be dissuaded from approaching a writer because of budget concerns. There are numerous ways to involve a writer, including consultancies aimed at providing feedback on narrative direction.

"Don't assume that because a writer has worked on AAA that they won't work on an indie game," Pratchett recommends. "I had some of my best experiences working on the Overlord games with Triumph Studios. It never hurts to ask. Especially if you think the writer would be well suited to your game. Also consider using writers for consultancy purposes. It can be a good way of milking their creative juices, without committing too much budget."

WHEN SHOULD I BRING A WRITER ONTO THE PROJECT?

Williams believes that a writer or narrative director should be brought on early in the process. This will likely lead to a more cohesive game in which exciting moments better serve the overarching vision.

"An experienced game writer who understands design is the best tool a creative director can have on a project," Williams explains. "They can see a project's big picture. Ultimately, a writer's job is to create logic where there is none – to make every arbitrary design choice appear as if it exists to serve a greater whole. This is much easier to accomplish when a writer or narrative director has been on the project from the beginning because they know what's come before, they're aware of the limitations, and they know what the team can accomplish."

Some writers prefer to begin work a little later. This gives the team time to get the pillars in place and provide a framework for the story.

"I am actually a writer that doesn't mind coming in a little bit after development has started, so that the team actually have an idea of what they want," Pratchett says. "They're not just randomly looking for someone to help, and they don't really know anything about the story, or what they want. That's much harder for me to get into, because I don't have as much time as I did when I first started out in the industry, because I'm doing other projects as well."

Pratchett suggests writers can also play a vital role early in a project. You may want to bring someone on to help flesh out your game concept.

"Keep in mind that writers can do a lot more than the word bits," Pratchett says. "A lot of what we can do is invisible work. It is the behind-the-scenes stuff like building the narratives of the world and looking at how the mechanics and the levels can support the narrative. It's a lot of world-building stuff. It can contribute to environmental storytelling. Ideally, with an experienced game writer, they'll be able to look at different aspects of your game and talk to you about how those can better support the narrative. The earlier you get a writer in on a project, the more they can help out."

That's not to say you need to keep a writer engaged consistently throughout the project. You can manage costs by bringing someone in for world-building for a short period of time and then re-engage them for the script and dialogue when ready.

"You'll find that what you need a writer to do will have peaks and troughs," Pratchett explains. "Just because you get a writer in early does not mean that they're going to be paid the same amount the entire way through the project, that they will be paid when they're doing a big load of work at the start. It's perfectly acceptable to get a writer in for a few days to look over your story documents. I've done that before in a consulting capacity, where I've just looked through the story documents and just drafted a whole load of notes. And you can use more established, more experienced writers. That's quite a good way of using them when you've got a little bit of budget to get their services for a couple of days. Just giving consultancy or feedback seems to prove very useful to people."

HOW DO WRITERS PRICE THEIR SERVICES?

As with most aspects of game development, pricing can vary significantly based on scope of work and the writer's experience. In order to understand what a game's story is going to cost, you must be able to communicate your needs.

Williams offers developers hourly, weekly, and monthly rates. Those are largely for budgeting convenience, as weekly and monthly options are derived from the hourly rate multiplied by time.

Writers often consider a variety of factors when quoting a rate. These include how far along development is and how quickly a writer must turn around the work.

"I charge less for concept and pre-production, because they are less time consuming, then I increase my rate when script writing begins," Williams says. "I will increase my rate based on scope vs. time. If you need a lot of writing done in a short amount of time, I will charge more, because it will be cutting into my personal life."

It's up to developers to determine how much work they need from a writer. You should consider creating a rough estimate for critical path script length and the number of systemic lines.

Williams suggests that many writers can comfortably produce five to fifteen script pages per day. For systemic line writing, anticipate a range between 50 and 200 lines per day.

From there, it's relatively easy to calculate how much time you'll need. Simply divide your total work by the middle-ground estimates. This gives you the basic time requirements for one draft. Writing rates can range from $50 to $100 per hour.

Many writers factor revisions into their process. A draft typically includes a full round of writing and incorporating one set of notes. Some writers might allow a second set of notes, if they are minor or due to the writer's error.

GETTING IT RIGHT

Revisions, which in other disciplines may be known as amendments, are something to be conscious of when reviewing a freelance contract. Costs can escalate quickly if you're constantly asking for revisions. Not to mention the frustration that can breed. When dealing with freelancers, have a plan and talk about it with them from the start. Measure twice, cut once. The budget will thank you.

Since writers work by the hour, your limit for rewrites and edits is based on your budget. If you're thorough with your requirements and smart about your notes, you can get more for your money.

"If you hire me on an hourly rate, I'll keep writing as long as you keep paying me," Williams says. "If you hire me for a week, I'll deliver a draft per week, plus a round of implementing notes. If you hire me for a full month, I'll give you as many revisions as you can cram into the allotted time."

Some developers might offer milestone-based pay. That can prove problematic, as delivery is often outside a writer's control.

"I shy away from milestones as a writer, because every time they've been in there, they have been broken by the company, and not me," Pratchett explains. "In one case, I hadn't been able to fulfill a milestone by months because of the company not being able to get me what I needed on time. So it's become easier and cleaner for me as a writer—though it might not necessarily be as useful for a developer—having a set day rate."

The Writers' Guild of Great Britain offers **guidelines (not mandatory minimums) for video game writers**[4]:

- Original material: £450+ ($625+) per day:
  This is work that involves the creation of a new/original IP.
  Intellectual property rights should also be considered in this case.
- Narrative/dialogue work: £350 - £450 ($500 - $650) per day:
  This is original writing, but within an IP not owned by/originated with the writer
- Localization, editing, copywriting: £300 - £350 ($425 to $500) per day: This is work that is focused more on polishing, requiring minimal rewriting.

While The Writers Guild of America (WGA) has not published guidelines of this nature, it does provide a **template contract for developers**[5]. The purpose of the contract is to enable writers to receive benefits employers contribute to the Producer-Writers Guild of America Pension Plan and the Writers Guild-Industry Health Fund.

[4] "Writing for Videogames," The Writers' Guild of Great Britain. July, 2015.
https://writersguild.org.uk/wp-content/uploads/2015/02/WGGB-A4-Videogames-2.pdf.
(accessed February 8, 2018).
[5] "Interactive Program Contract for Videogames," WGA.org.
http://www.wga.org/contracts/contracts/other-contracts/interactive-program-contract.
(accessed February 8, 2018).

Unlike the Screen Actors Guild - American Federation of Television and Radio Artists (SAG-AFTRA), the WGA does not have a negotiated contract with developers and publishers. There are no union-mandated minimum rates when working with a WGA member, giving developers and writers freedom to negotiate.

"Most writers will have some wiggle room," Pratchett says. "In the past when I've worked on smaller games, we have come to some arrangement about pay versus bonus for sales. I'd say it's possible to negotiate with most writers, but you have to be aware that the more experienced the writer, the more expensive they're likely to be. But the Writers' Guild guidelines are a good ballpark both for developers, to know what they're getting into, and for writers to give them a guideline. You can bet the more experienced writers will be much more expensive than that."

WHAT SHOULD BE IN A WRITER'S CONTRACT?

The best contracts are those that explicitly detail both parties' rights and obligations. In addition to the standard clauses, writing contracts typically include a number of provisions.

These include:

CREDIT

Before you begin working with a writer, you should consider how you'll recognize their work. There may be reasons you don't want to (or can't) credit everyone that contributes to the narrative. Whatever you choose, it should be communicated clearly in the contract. You don't want this to be a dispute later.

EXCLUSIVITY

Some developers consider themselves to be in close competition with others. You might not be able to get the writer you want, because they've been contractually prohibited from working on games that might compete with one another. You might also consider an exclusivity clause, but you'll need to woo your chosen writer in other ways.

KILL POINTS

This isn't the express domain of writing contracts, but the ability to terminate the contract without penalty is important here. Typically, writer contracts include the provision for either party to end the relationship at certain milestones. You might realize during the concept or pre-production phase, for example, that a writer isn't the best fit for your project. It might be better to part ways as friends rather than stretch out a difficult working relationship.

PRESS RELATIONS NEEDS

A game's story is sometimes used as a key promotional point. In those cases, you might want to ensure that your writer will make themselves available to speak with the press or appear at events.

IN THIS CHAPTER, WE LEARNED....

1. How to prepare appropriately before finding a narrative designer or writer.
2. Different ways writers work with developers.
3. What you should include in a writer's contract.

CHAPTER
SEVEN

HOW MUCH DOES VOICE ACTING COST?

We've come a long way since *Resident Evil's* "master of unlocking" and "Jill sandwich." Voice acting is common in today's games, and the talent available is quite astounding. If you ever want to be overwhelmed by the richness that's out there, spend an afternoon on YouTube searching for voice actors practicing their craft and enjoy the show.

Your game might very well thrive without acting or performance capture. If you're considering either (or both) of those elements, you'll want to have a good sense of costs. You'll also want to make sure you make these decisions early enough in your timeline, so voiceover doesn't hold up your release.

HOW DO I FIND VOICE ACTORS FOR MY GAME?

One thing we learned as we talked to professionals in different disciplines is that open auditions can cost you more time than you could ever want to spend (see Chapter 5). The same is true for voice acting. The option is there, and you may want to roll the dice, but your results are going to be varied.

"The cheapest option is putting up your audition materials on a website like voices.com," says actress Ashly Burch (*Life is Strange, Horizon: Zero Dawn*). "The drawback with this option is that you're going to get tons of auditions, which sounds like a great thing initially. Ask anyone who has cast something before—it gets real tedious... and real overwhelming... real quick—and you're also going to get a wide variance in skill level. There will be some folks on there that have never acted before and/or aren't trained—which might be totally fine—but also might be challenging if you aren't an experienced director."

If you want to take a more focused approach, you can identify actors you'd like to use based on their other work. At that point, you'll need to contact their agents. Many of these individuals are part of the Screen Actors Guild - American Federation of Television and Radio Artists (SAG-AFTRA).

While it's more expensive to work with union actors, that pool isn't just for big-budget games. SAG-AFTRA has been working toward a low budget agreement that would help indies access bigger talent.

Many games featuring union talent are recorded in Los Angeles, California. The agencies in that city (Abrams Artists, SBV, CESD, DPN, and Atlas) are a good starting point. Before you contact them, you'll want to have **sides**[1] prepared.

If you aren't located in Los Angeles, you can watch your recording session and provide notes to actors via Skype. Costs can also be controlled in other ways.

---

[1] **Sides** - A document containing all the information an actor might need for a role. This includes the character's name, race, age, personality description, preferred vocal range, and references (for instance a specific actor's voice). Sides also include an audition script. This should be a short scene. If you require different emotions, you may opt for two or three short scenes or lines of dialog.

"There are many actors that will have their own home studio setups," Burch advises. "You can even state in the sides that you will only consider actors with a home studio, if that's important for your budget."

If contacting agencies seems like a daunting task, specific actors might be able to refer you to their agents for guidance on the process. Some agents can also advise on making your project SAG-eligible.

"If you know you want to use a particular union actor, try reaching out to their agent directly," Burch suggests. "We're more accessible than you think! If the actor digs your project and wants to be involved, they might help you by contacting SAG on your behalf so that you can get the ball rolling a bit faster and easier. I've offered this to a couple of indies already."

For those developers that have some additional financial wherewithal, a signatory might be a good hire. These professionals handle SAG compliance and casting. Some will even direct recording sessions on your behalf.

WHAT DO I NEED TO KNOW ABOUT UNION CONTRACTS?

If you're working with union actors, you'll need to adhere to safety and compensation protocols. Here are some things to consider:

- Union rates are minimums. While you may have an actor's agent seek additional compensation depending on the project, you won't be able to get away with less.

- Following a lengthy strike, SAG-AFTRA ratified a new, **three-year contract with publishers in 2016**[2]. This includes secondary compensation (royalties) based on number of units sold or subscribers. This amount is 25 percent of a session fee, capping out at four sessions. The maximum secondary fee for actors is $3,302.00, though there is a discount if you pre-pay the royalty when you hire the actor. Otherwise, the payment will be due no later than the game's launch. Yes, this means you have to guess how many units you'll sell or subscribers you'll attract.

[2] "SAG-AFTRA 2016 Video Game Agreements," SAGAFTRA.org. https://www.sagaftra.org/files/2016_video_game_agreement_0.pdf. (accessed January 10, 2018).

- Sessions with actors are booked in either two- or four-hour increments. Breaks are required every hour.

- Voice actors can record no more than four hours per session. During that time, an actor may perform no more than three different characters.

- Recording incidental lines should be limited to two hours per session. This is often strenuous work and should be scheduled for the end of a session. Incidental lines often include grunts, yells, and pain sounds. Skilled actors can usually nail these in one take. You shouldn't ask for more than two, especially if these are full-throated screams lasting multiple seconds.

- Non-disclosure agreements are handled separately from the union contract. You'll want to have these prepared by your attorney. Actors know not to talk about projects they're working on without permission from the developer or publisher, but sometimes performers slip up. This can potentially disrupt your big surprise months (or years) **before you're ready**[3].

FINDING TALENT IN UNEXPECTED PLACES

Sometimes, the best actor for the job is hiding in plain sight. When Ninja Theory began work on *Hellblade: Senua's Sacrifice*, it set out to make a AAA-quality game on a smaller budget.

The studio began its ambitious performance capture work, but didn't use a casting agency as it usually does. Ninja Theory's cinematics lead Steve Manship explains why the title role went to Melina Juergens, the studio's video editor turned **BAFTA-winning performer**[4].

At the beginning of the project, while looking for someone to fill the role, we had lots of tests we needed to do as we looked into building our own mocap stage in the office and doing our own performance capture in-house. Melina always had to be the stand in and as things progressed and the tests became more and more complex, turning into small acted out scenes, her suitability for the role became more and more evident.

Also, on Hellblade *we were looking to do things a different way than previous games. We didn't want to book a four to five week block at an external mocap studio and capture everything we thought we needed there and then. We wanted more flexibility, so we wanted to bring it all in house so we could shoot whenever we needed to, relatively simply. Having an actor on call with that kind of flexibility, for a project lasting a few years would have been very difficult, if not impossible.*

This need, combined with Melina's clearly developing abilities, led to many discussions about the best way forward and eventually, to Melina's casting as Senua. Obviously we're all very happy with how that turned out, she did an awesome job.

4   "British Academy Games Awards in 2018," BAFTA.org. April 12, 2018.
       http://www.bafta.org/games/awards/games-awards-2018. (accessed April 12, 2018).

WHO DIRECTS A VOICE ACTING SESSION?

Professional actors can do a good job with a well-written script, but a director's guidance will often tease out a better performance. Sometimes you'll want to have a seasoned director guiding the recording session, though this is an additional cost.

In some cases, developers choose to manage their own voice acting sessions. There are different approaches to this, so consider what you want from the session.

"It's no small task and can be difficult, but there's no right or wrong way. You could have a very clear and solid idea of what you want or no idea at all and be more open to input," says Steven Manship, cinematics lead at Ninja Theory (*DmC: Devil May Cry, Hellblade: Senua's Sacrifice*). "So essentially it comes down to the developer and what level of input you want to have and expect from the people you choose to work with. You can expect to be working closely with someone though so try to find someone you think you can work with, as well as someone who'll bring what you need to the role. In my experience actors I've worked with have always been professional and very eager to do the absolute best they can so it's nothing to be afraid of, and finding the right person can bring so much more to the experience than you knew you needed."

This has the potential to be extremely productive, but can also inhibit success. Be sure you understand the challenges that directing recording sessions can bring.

"Often, when I'm working with independent developers, they choose to direct their own projects," Burch says. "That's totally fine and can often be an enjoyable experience, but it's important to be aware that this is a profession that some people dedicate their entire lives to, so it isn't something that will necessarily be very easy and natural to pick up. If you haven't studied directing, hiring a seasoned director is a wonderful option if you have money available for that purpose."

Burch offers the following tips for those who want to direct recording sessions on their own:

I. UNDERSTAND YOUR CHARACTER

This might seem obvious, but you'd be surprised how many folks have amazing designs for their characters and epic battle mechanics, but have no idea who that person actually is. It doesn't have to be incredibly elaborate, depending on the project - if you need your orc to be angry and violent and that's all you need, easy peasy. But really know your character, and be able to describe them succinctly and concretely. Creating sides is a great exercise to see how quickly and clearly you can communicate your intention with a character.

2. KNOW WHAT INFORMATION TO CONVEY ABOUT YOUR CHARACTER.

If you're not going to provide the script to an actor before they record, then you'll need to convey pertinent information to them during the session. If you give them too much information, they may lose the thread of what is truly important for them to focus on. Not only that, you're wasting time that you could be using to record. If you give them no information, they might be able to piece things together from context clues, or they might be completely lost at sea. Personally, I like knowing the plot details that pertain to my character, how I feel about the characters I'm interacting with—this is a big one—and any brief, relevant details from my backstory.

3. TRUST YOUR ACTOR

While you should understand the core of who your character is, you are hiring a particular actor because you agreed with or were inspired by their interpretation of your character. So make it a true collaboration and allow them to play within the space that you've established. By that I mean: don't come into the session with a very specific way that every line should be said and not allow any deviation from that plan. I mean, you can do that, but the performance you get isn't going to be as compelling or feel as organic. You hired this person for a reason, so trust yourself for choosing them and trust their expertise as a performer. And if you're a bit squeamish about giving trust - I get that! This is your baby and you're afraid someone else is going to drop it. That's what callbacks are for! If you need to be rigorous in the casting process so that you can trust the actor in the booth, then do so. But once they're in, give them the trust they've earned and deserve.

4. MAKE YOUR DIRECTION CONCISE

This goes double if your actor is in an emotional place. If you wax poetic about the scene and the character, you run the risk of the actor losing the moment they're in and the thread of what you're saying. Be direct and short - use adjectives more than analogies - and try to get them back in the moment.

5. DECIDE HOW YOU WANT TO MOVE THROUGH THE SCRIPT.

This is more technical, but useful to think about. Do you want the actor to do 3 takes of a line before you give them feedback? Do you want the actor to perform an entire scene? Or maybe a chunk of a scene? Are you going to read the other character(s) with them as they perform? It's also completely acceptable to ask the actor's preference if you don't have one yourself. I actually kind of like it when directors do that, because it makes me feel like they're more open to collaboration.

HOW LONG WILL I NEED IN THE RECORDING STUDIO?

It can be challenging figuring out how long your script will take to record, especially if you've never done this before. There are a few ways to approach this, though.

"If you're hiring a sound studio for the recording, speak to them and give them the script," Manship says. "They should be able to give you a good idea of the required time. Read through the script yourself, out loud, and time it. Take into account you will need to record each line at least two or three times for safety, more if you struggle to find the performance you need."

Once you're in the studio, time required can vary. You'll need to consider whether a number of factors when budgeting recording sessions.

"It comes down to the complexity of the script and the depth of the performance," Manship explains. "You may choose to have a day or half day rehearsal with the actor. This will help a lot and is recommended. Better to block it all out while just paying a fee for their time rather than the full costs involved in using a sound studio. From a rehearsal day, you should be able to get a very good estimation of the time you'll need, and you could have the

performance nailed, or at least be closer to it. Bear in mind even if you're happy with the performance you'll still need the extra takes for safety. Another note, if you're recording the actors as a group or individually will also matter. A group recording can get a more lifelike and dynamic recording session but may take more time. Definitely do rehearsal days if choosing to go that route."

WHAT ABOUT PERFORMANCE CAPTURE?

Sometimes, you want more than just an actor's voice. Adding motion and performance capture to your game might be outside your budget right now, but technology is evolving at breakneck speed. As you grow and tech becomes more attainable, you may be able to consider these things faster than you might expect.

In addition to increased fees for actors, you're going to need space and technology. Costs can vary greatly based on the type of space you'll use.

"Actors perform in what's called a volume—a large space set up specifically for motion capture," Burch says. "I've also worked in relatively smaller set ups. Talent is generally paid more for performance capture, because it's a more intensive process and performance capture usually lasts the full day."

There are a number of considerations when picking a performance space. Manship offers the following guidance:

- How many actors are required on the stage simultaneously?
- How many motion capture cameras will you need?
- Are your actors in Los Angeles? Will you use a studio there or fly actors to you for capture?
- Are you capturing in-game animations? Will you need enough space to capture a full sprint cycle? Do you need high ceiling space for climbs or swinging weapons?

"All these need to be taken into account before you make the decision where to shoot the mocap for your games," Manship says. "If using a mocap studio then who fits best? Should you use one at all, or use your budget to set up a space for yourself and do it all in-house? Do you have staff capable of running a shoot and processing mocap data? Do you have a suitable space?"

ONE STUDIO, TWO APPROACHES TO PERFORMANCE CAPTURE

Ninja Theory has used motion capture extensively in its most recent games, *DmC: Devil May Cry* and *Hellblade: Senua's Sacrifice*. The studio tackled these challenges differently during the projects, as each game required different resources.

Cinematic lead Steve Manship shared the following stories about performance capture for those games.

We made DmC: Devil May Cry *for an external publisher and were given a substantial mocap cinematic budget. We had multiple characters and hired five actors, all based in LA. The game was a western take and was set in the US.*

At any one time we knew we'd have three to four characters in the shooting space acting together in the same scene. We also knew we wanted to capture multiple cameras in the same space so we could edit between them, so this meant another two to three bodies in the space shooting the action with cable wranglers. All these bodies mean more mocap camera views can be blocked and the data compromised. Therefore, we knew we needed a very large shooting space with massive amount of mocap cameras and people with expertise handling a shoot of this size and all the data it would generate.

We were doing full performance capture—so body, facial and audio capture all at the same time – and would need all of the relevant equipment for that many actors on hand. We had a locked-down script and estimated we needed four weeks of shooting time in one block to get everything captured that we needed.

When we took all these factors into account along with our budget the best option was to hire an external studio based in LA with a good track record—in this case Giant Studios.

Hellblade: Senua's Sacrifice *was an internal project, an original IP, self-funded with a small budget and small team—20 people average. Only one main, performance-captured character, in scenes that were very confined. The style of the game was to be a one-shot experience with no cuts, so we only wanted to capture one camera in the shoots.*

This meant we only ever had to have two people in the shooting space at any time and was the opposite situation to DmC. We only needed a small space and a much smaller amount of mocap cameras, plus we only needed the facial recording and audio hardware for one actor. Our actor was local and always on hand, and we wanted to take full advantage of the flexibility that comes with that.

We flat out didn't have the budget to use an external mocap studio but after reaching out to Vicon found that a suitable set could be built in-house for our budget in our main meeting room, and given the stylistic choices that had been made and the staff we have here we could do it ourselves and capture data that was as good as any we got externally. So it was a no-brainer for us.

So, there's no right or wrong. Those two examples show the kinds of questions you need to ask of your project, and from that you can make a decision that's right for you in that situation.

IN THIS CHAPTER,
WE LEARNED....

I.   How to budget for voice actors.
2.   What you'll need to consider when working
      with union actors.
3.   What you need for performance capture.

CHAPTER
EIGHT

WHAT'S THE BEST WAY TO WORK WITH PR?

The romantics will say, "If only it were still easy enough to simply make your game, not put any effort into promotion and live off the sales on Steam and consoles, we'd never have to market our game and adoption rates would approach 100 percent."

OK. Let's be real. It was never "simple" even when discoverability wasn't a Herculean challenge. Where the challenge for independent developers once was even getting on Steam or consoles, now it's standing out from their peers. And having a good game isn't good enough. Heck, having a great game, in many cases, isn't good enough anymore.

Today, it can be positively frightening to launch a game. Chances are you're competing with a hundred or more new titles, let alone those that are just a week or two old. This is not an exaggeration. 2017 saw an **average of 21 games released on Steam every day**[1]. EVERY. DAY.

We are entering a new era of challenge for independent developers. The floodgates are now open on digital distribution networks and potential customers are inundated with choices.

You need to stand out in the crowd. One of the best ways to do that is to have someone on your team (either internal or contracted) handling press and public relations, including community development.

WHAT WILL A PR PROFESSIONAL OR AGENCY DO FOR ME?

Regardless of how you work with a PR professional or how much work they do for you, the goal is the same: generate publicity. This broad perspective includes a variety of tasks and approaches to reach the finish line.

Some companies might be more comfortable teasing out interesting stories from smaller games and studios. Other PR professionals might know how to make the most of big licenses and bigger budgets to make a huge media splash.

"Exactly how a company generates publicity—both in terms of the services they offer and the approach they take—will vary from one company to the next," says Evolve PR founder Tom Ohle. "Certain agencies are more comfortable gaining mainstream media attention, while others focus on influencer engagement; some may take an old-school approach and rely heavily on press releases, while others may think that your presence at events—PAX, E3 and the like—are the best way to connect to media and influencers; one agency may focus on grassroots activities to build buzz from the ground up, while another reckons that securing high-profile media coverage will trickle attention downward."

[1]   Sinclair, Brandon. "Steam saw more than 7,600 games debut in 2017," *GamesIndustry.biz.* January 10, 2018. https://www.gamesindustry.biz/articles/2018-01-10-steam-saw-more-than-7-600-games-debut-in-2017-steamspy. (accessed February 20, 2018.)

Many PR professionals and agencies offer supplementary and complementary services in order to get the most traction. These can include:

- Media training - It's important to stay on topic while giving a demo or interview to the press. Media training can also help hone your message and selling points.
- Event demos - PAX, GDC, and E3 are important showcase opportunities, even if you aren't on the show floor. PR professionals can help coordinate your presence and book press to see your game.
- On-site demos - Sometimes it's easier for press to demo your game if you visit them. Desk-side presentations are common, and you'll probably want help setting them up.
- Reputation building - Speaking at PAX, GDC, and other events can help raise your profile. Some PR agencies can help book speaking engagements.
- Crisis planning - Controversy can catch even the most prepared team by surprise. Having a plan for dealing with challenging moments is the best way to survive an unfortunate incident.

Some agencies, like Evolve PR, offer additional services to help shepherd a game through launch and beyond. "We also supplement those core services with marketing and social media-focused activities, as we feel that modern PR requires a holistic approach," Ohle explains. "Everything you do to promote your game should be planned with all potential areas—PR, advertising, marketing, social media—in mind."

DON'T SKIP MEDIA TRAINING

Even if you don't hire PR professionals to run your entire campaign, don't make the mistake of ignoring media training. You know the the story about the dev who stuck his foot in his mouth. Yeah, that one. The really bad one.

Did you have too many to choose from in your mind to figure out exactly which one we're referring to? Of course you did. That's because almost every incident you can mention when a dev made headlines or caused a Twitter scandal had to do with a lack of media training.

Media training is about clear, focused messaging about your game. If you comment about the industry in general, you better make sure you know how to talk without getting yourself in trouble.

We're not saying you shouldn't be a participant in the bigger industry conversations. It's important to engage your peers and be part of these discussions.

What we are saying is that this is a learned skill. It requires practice. And if you aren't naturally deft with your words, you should seek out a professional to help you prepare for interviews and craft your social media presence. You don't want to be a casualty of bungled language in a public social media post.

HOW DO I FIND THE RIGHT PR AGENCY?

Not all PR pros and shops are the same. Some focus exclusively on entertainment instead of taking on a wider range of clients. Others build strong relationships with enthusiast press instead of mainstream.

"The different approaches are worth considering as you think about which agency to partner with," Ohle says. "A company that's been doing a lot of PR for major corporations may not be comfortable 'getting dirty' with an indie game, while an influencer-focused team may have no clue how to land a big media story."

Some publishers engage multiple PR shops with different expertise. There might be a contract for mainstream media, another for enthusiast outlets, and another for influencer relations.

"Ask friends and colleagues for references," suggests Stride PR founder Robert Brown. "If another developer gives an agency a strong endorsement, then you'll know they did something right."

Brown also suggests asking an agency a number of questions to determine fit:

- What projects has the agency been proud to work on?
- Does the agency work with smaller independent developers?
- How long has your contact at the agency worked in PR?
- How involved will the person selling the services be with your account? You might be speaking to the head of the agency, but your account might be assigned a junior staff member. Find out the experience level of the person representing you to the media.

When looking for a PR professional, you're interviewing the person who is going to be on the front lines of your relationship with the press. A personality fit is a must, as is engaging someone that has proven experience meeting goals similar to yours.

"Talk to every agency or freelancer you can, and figure out which one will be the best fit for your needs," Ohle suggests. "Know which territories you want covered—a UK-based agency may not have great contacts with North American press, and vice versa—which press or influencers you want to reach, and what you'd consider a successful campaign. The more you know about what you want, the easier it will be to see if an agency can meet your needs."

WHEN DURING DEVELOPMENT SHOULD I ENGAGE PR?

There's no hard and fast rule that dictates when you should hire a PR company for your in-development game. The answer depends on genre, platform, and scope.

"For most mobile game releases, I wouldn't suggest contacting press until a couple weeks before launch," Brown recommends. "On the other hand, the very latest you would want to start with a console or PC game launch is four to six weeks before launch. With those timelines in mind, it is also important to remember that an agency is going to need a few more weeks lead time to prepare."

Some agencies can assist during the prototype phase. It's their job to have a broad view of the industry and trends. Take advantage of that experience.

"I always encourage developers to talk with agencies while prototyping different concepts to get a sense of which ideas will get the press most excited," Brown advises. Ohle concurs, suggesting that PR agencies and professionals can help give developers an idea of what will sell (and what won't).

"I don't think it's ever too early to engage a PR team or freelancer," he says. "A PR team will, ideally, help you to actually understand what makes your game sellable—something so important I can't possibly understate. If you don't have a clear hook that will appeal to your audience—whether that's press, influencers, or gamers in general—you're going to struggle to get attention down the line; if you can recognize that challenge before you've even announced your game, you can save yourself a lot of grief. You need to be thinking about a ton of different ways your game might appeal to players, how to showcase those game elements effectively, which press and influencers to approach, when best to approach them, etc. It's always better to get that sorted out early than to wait until the last minute, only to find out that your game doesn't have strong appeal, you're launching head-to-head with a AAA game, nobody's heard about it yet, and you don't have any cool trailers planned. That's not fun."

DON'T UNDERBUDGET FOR MARKETING AND PR

While there's no scientific equation that can spin marketing budget into game sales, you do get what you pay for. Unless you're making your game as a hobby project, the goal is for people to play and love your hard work.

In order to get to that point, you'll need to convince your potential players that your game is worth buying. In order for them to even consider purchasing, they need to be aware your game exists.

"'How much should we budget?'" is one of the hardest questions to answer when developers start talking to us about services," Ohle says. "I think that conventional wisdom suggests that you want to put somewhere between 20 and 50 percent of your production budget to marketing. Most indie devs start screaming and flailing when those sorts of numbers are thrown around, and we routinely have developers come to us, having spent three years of their lives making a game and expecting to get massive attention with a $5,000 marketing budget. Sure, it's possible to succeed with a modest budget and a good amount of hard work, but it's probably not the best way to go about minimizing your risk of failure."

Both Ohle and Brown suggest that you could spend thousands per month on an agency with a proven track record. Expect to pay between $1,000 and $10,000 per month for a freelancer or agency. For many established independent developers, $4,000 per month is a reasonable budget. Ohle urges developers to spend an amount with which they are comfortable. You just need to be realistic about what you'll get if you're marketing on a shoestring.

"When a developer approaches us with a set budget, we really try to understand how we could best put that budget to use," Ohle explains. "While we always suggest using up a good chunk of available time to develop the initial promotional plan and strategy, from there it's pretty much wide open. Sometimes we're involved on an ongoing basis with a monthly fee, helping with anything and everything that pops up; sometimes we help develop the strategy and then go quiet for a few months, before popping up to help push an important announcement; in other cases we just jump in and help secure coverage around launch. How much—and how—an agency needs to be involved will often depend on a developer's internal capabilities. If a developer is comfortable preparing announcements, that's time we can spend on something else; if they just need an extra set of hands to send out review codes, we can do that."

It's also important to consider other costs that go beyond campaign planning, production, and management. These include:

- Show attendance - Ohle suggests budgeting $8,000 for a small presence on the PAX show floor, with larger shows and booths increasing the cost drastically.
- Press tours
- Promotional mailings (t-shirts, collectibles)
- Trailer production (see below)
- Influencer campaigns - These can cost between $1,000 and $100,000 per video, depending on who you're working with.
- Social media pushes
- Advertising

"Developers have a breadth of options when exploring different ways to work with an agency, from a project basis for an approaching launch or trade show, to a monthly retainer for a big upcoming release or a studio with multiple games in the pipeline," Brown says. "In most cases, a developer doesn't need to go on retainer, so explore your options if a PR firm suggests it."

THE ROMANCE AND REALITY OF THE "OVERNIGHT SUCCESS"

For many developers, delivering an "indie darling" isn't about wads of cash pouring into your bank account (though that is a nice feeling). It's about people playing and loving your heartfelt creation (and earning enough to make your next game).

In *The GameDev Business Handbook*, we took on the notion of the "overnight success" developer and pointed out how the vast majority of these stories don't acknowledge the numerous AAA and AA games those devs launched before going independent. It's not a romantic story.

The same holds true for many hit independent games. First, take a look and see if one of those runaway hits has a publisher. In many cases, they are benefitting from a publisher's institutional knowledge, prior relationships, and street credibility with audiences. Publishers already have reach into the gaming community on social media, via mailing lists, and (of course) with the press.

It's possible that a publisher isn't in play. In that case, see if the developer has a marketing partner assisting with outreach.

The idea that a game "came out of nowhere" is a romantic story for devs, games, and life. In most cases, "nowhere" is a set of conditions that were created by smart people with resources at their disposal. While it certainly is possible for the exceedingly rare perfect storm to create critical mass for an unknown title from an unheard of developer, very little actually happens in a vacuum.

I WANT A FLASHY TRAILER SO HOW MUCH IS THAT GOING TO COST ME?

Think of the best trailers you've ever seen. Did they change the way you felt about a game? Were you introduced to a new franchise thanks to engaging, short-form storytelling?

Great trailers can set the tone for your entire marketing campaign. An unknown title can be catapulted into the gaming zeitgeist with just a minute or two of video. In fact, you might not even show gameplay at all, opting for what amounts to a tone-setting short film (the first *Dead Island* trailer comes to mind).

You can always cut a trailer yourself with accessible video editing tools, but you'll likely see greater impact from working with a professional. This is another area that can conform to your comfort level. While publishers can spend huge on a trailer, you can also have one made for a much more accessible amount. And whether you're the biggest publisher in the world or the tiniest bedroom dev, you're going to find a majority of your traction on social media.

"Producing a great trailer takes a keen eye, expertise, and a lot of time," Ohle says. "A lot of trailers are produced for more than $100,000. A more modest budget would be between $5,000 and $20,000 for a single trailer. Of course, there are ways to reduce costs—hiring a single freelancer is usually cheaper than bringing on a full-service agency; a gameplay video costs a lot less than a custom CG sequence; and using an unknown artist's music is going to be cheaper than licensing a Led Zeppelin track, etc.—but you don't want to skimp here."

You can get the most bang for your buck by reusing pieces of the video throughout your campaign. Ohle suggests cutting your big trailer into smaller, quick hit videos. "Try to repurpose assets when possible, he says. "Cut a handful of short, social-media-focused trailers out of a larger one, for instance."

LIKE, COMMENT, AND SUBSCRIBE

The process of communicating with gamers has undergone a massive shift as social media and video platforms have become mainstream. Video game media used to be the gatekeeper, first in print, and then online.

With the advent of YouTube, Twitch, and other video platforms, unaffiliated influencers have developed rapt audiences of hungry game consumers. Unlike traditional media, you may need to pay these individuals for placement (this can include late night television appearances, like Conan O'Brien's "Clueless Gamer" segment). Other influencers make coverage decisions closer to traditional outlets, basing content on audience interest rather than a pay-to-play model. There's still an unspoken hierarchy even among streamers. If a popular streamer sees traction from a game, the next tier and the next tier and the next tier will follow. Efforts are best focused on streamers who try new games.

Rates vary significantly. As stated above, you can anticipate fees ranging from $1,000 to $100,000 per video depending on a variety of factors, including the influencer's reach. Note that many countries have guidelines governing how paid promotions are disclosed to viewers.

Transparency is crucial. Even if you aren't directly risking a fine for improper or missing disclosures, you can take a public relations hit just by being involved with a non-compliant influencer. Be sure that whomever you decide to work with understands and complies with disclosure rules.

HOW DO I KNOW IF MY PUBLIC RELATIONS EFFORTS ARE WORKING?

Many of the people you work with will produce work you can easily evaluate. The same isn't true of public and press relations.

Public relations professionals use "key performance indicators" (KPIs) to convey impact of their work. However, the source data is often challenging to work with, because many of the metrics are quantity driven rather than measuring the quality of impressions.

"The number of media mentions in a given timeframe seems like a nice number to look at, I suppose, but doesn't say much about the quality of those articles," Ohle explains. "Number of article shares via social media seems like a promising way to measure impact, until you realize just how many bots are out there retweeting every story posted to major media outlets—again, quality is tough to determine. 'Share of voice' can be helpful, comparing how many times your game has been mentioned when compared to competitive titles, though again, the numbers themselves don't really speak to the quality of the content, or the sentiment therein."

There are qualitative measures, though the data leading to those is significantly more difficult to gather. The trade-off might help you hone your approach to public relations and marketing, though.

"Analyzing sentiment and audience engagement (comments on articles, shares, etc.) are good measures, though effectively analyzing potentially hundreds or thousands of articles and videos can be very time-consuming," Ohle explains. "Driving traffic to a store page or official site can be a great measure of success—as can direct sales data—but on the agency side we rarely get access to that data."

In other words, you'll need to keep an eye on some PR activities that require storefront access in order to determine results. Ultimately, Ohle suggests that you set reasonable, measurable goals for each of your initiatives.

These can include:

- Attendance at a trade show/community event (E3, PAX, etc.) can be measured by number of people visiting your booth.
- Game launch PR and marketing can be gauged by number of reviews, critical response (Metacritic, OpenCritic), video views, and sales.

"The best approach is to set your own goals," Ohle says. "Determine what you want out of a campaign—and work with your PR or marketing team to reach them."

Just remember that PR is one piece of the puzzle. Other games releasing in your launch window and the quality of your game play a huge role in determining awareness and sales.

"PR practitioners can't control everything, and goals should be set with that in mind," Ohle says. "Expecting your PR agency to only secure reviews with scores above 80 percent is kind of nuts. While we can send review units only to those media and influencers we think are most likely to enjoy a game, their actual opinions of the game aren't in our control."

BUDGETING FOR LIVE AND SERVICE-BASED GAMES

If your game is significantly or entirely online, your PR plans will rely on building and maintaining a community. A big piece of that is content updates and communications around those new features.

Rocket League developer Psyonix is an example of a company doing live game public relations right. PR and events manager Stephanie Thoensen offers some guidance on planning for PR when launch is only the beginning.

Planning PR for a game that will receive continuous updates requires additional budget on an ongoing basis dependent on the scope of the updates to the game. You have to assume there will be at least one or two trade shows or events each year that you'll need to have a presence at to either preview or debut some of the larger new content.

Additionally, depending on the cadence of content coming out, you need to plan enough PR support to make multiple announcements a year. If your game has a competitive or esports aspect, that also throws in another set of announcements and PR on-site support for major tournaments.

You will still need to invest a large amount of budget in the initial PR campaign of the game leading to the initial launch, but then keep in mind a smaller annual budget to support all ongoing activities.

"Community first" has always been a part of our mission statement and interacting with our community on a regular basis is quite important to us and the game. This has allowed us to build up and maintain a large community, as we take their feedback into consideration to update the game and make it better over time.

The costs involved aren't really costs in a traditional, monetary sense, but you have to ensure you have all of the right internal and external employees in place to support the community accordingly. As the community continues to grow, it often introduces the need for additional systems or external partners that weren't needed in the beginning and that's when additional monetary costs may come in.

When the game has an esports or competitive aspect to it, it adds in an entire other arm of PR support and cost that is needed. Often times it is on a similar schedule to regular game content updates and announcements, so there could be a need for a separate PR team or person to handle it. It adds a need to be flexible and strategic when scheduling all announcements in order to make sure everything exists harmoniously. There is also the additional cost in terms of time and travel to attend the major tournaments in order to line up interviews with players as well as any personalities that make sense for the specific tournament on-site. For a successful game with multiple tournaments, the esports element adds in almost as much support separately as the game itself.

The main difference between traditional games and live games is that planning and distributing announcements never ends with a live game. With a traditional release you plan a PR campaign that really begins with the announcement of the game and will eventually end once DLC launches or the game is in stores and no additional content will be added. A live game PR strategy is basically never ending, and each year almost acts as a new game campaign, or more so each large content update acts as such. Your PR strategy also adjusts down to a smaller scale once the initial launch is done and you move more into live service. You also have to take into consideration the scale of each of your updates when planning PR, as for us we mainly put more work into promoting larger feature updates and some that just have basic content don't have too much of a PR push.

IN THIS CHAPTER, WE LEARNED....

1	Different ways to work with PR professionals.
2	How to budget for PR efforts.
3	How to measure if your PR work is effective.

CHAPTER NINE

HOW DO I BUDGET FOR ALL THE SOFTWARE I NEED TO MAKE MY GAME?

Making your game isn't just about filling your skill positions and letting everyone go to work. People are a huge piece of your project budget, but you'll also need to make sure your employees have the necessary tools to accomplish their tasks.

We've compiled budgeting tips on some of the most commonly used tools in game development. Please note that costs and fee structures may change.

ENGINES

Unless you are a massive AAA publisher, you probably aren't going to be building your own engine. And if you are planning to build your own engine, is it really the best use of your time? For the majority of devs out there, you'll be licensing someone else's technology to power your game. There are a number of considerations when picking an engine, including functionality, ease of use, cost, royalty structure, and platform compatibility.

Each competitor handles its fee structure differently. Here are some things to consider for two of the most widely used engines:

UNREAL ENGINE (CREATED BY EPIC GAMES):

- Free to download.
- Royalty is set at 5 percent of gross revenue for any earnings more than $3,000 in a calendar quarter.
- Custom licenses are available for those who want to pay more up front to reduce royalty burden. Those are handled under non-disclosure agreement and should be discussed directly with Epic Games.
- End User License Agreement (EULA) must **"explicitly disclaim any representations, warranties, conditions, and liabilities related to the Unreal Engine."**[1]
- Proper crediting is required, with specific language set out by Epic Games.
- If using the Unreal Engine branding or logos, Epic requires developers comply with usage guidelines. An **explicit license**[2] is required.
- Your game must adhere to all local laws.
- You may not ship the Unreal editor or tools (or those derived from Unreal) to the general public.

Epic requires that developers **self-report earnings**[3] for royalty payment purposes. Note that any advance payments you receive for development, including publisher funding, are subject to the 5 percent royalty. These funds are due at the end of the quarter you receive them, not after your game ships. You'll only need to pay these fees

---

[1] "Unreal Engine 4 Commercial Game Development Guidelines," UnrealEngine.com. https://www.unrealengine.com/en-US/release. (accessed January 24, 2018).
[2] "Unreal Engine Branding Guidelines and Trademark Usage," UnrealEngine.com. https://www.unrealengine.com/branding. (accessed January 24, 2018).
[3] "How do I submit a royalty report for my UE4 project?" EpicGames.com. http://help.epicgames.com/customer/en/portal/articles/2313883-how-do-i-submit-a-royalty-report-for-my-ue4-project-?b_id=9727. (accessed January 24, 2018).

once, so you won't need to do so while your publisher recoups its investment. (*The GameDev Business Handbook* explains the details and structures of a recoup in Chapter 6.)

UNITY

Unity is the other widely used third-party engine. Unlike Unreal Engine, Unity is royalty-free. Instead, the engine licensing is handled on a per-user basis.

A free option (**Unity Personal**[4]) is available for students, hobbyists, and companies with under $100,000 of annual gross revenue. The next tier, **Unity Plus**[5], is available for studios with gross annual revenue up to $200,000. The $35 per seat per month fee includes additional services, including a customizable splash screen (instead of the default Unity splash), performance reporting, analytics, and software developer kits for ads and in-app purchases.

The top tier, **Unity Pro**[6], covers studios with gross annual revenues of greater than $200,000. The per seat per month cost increases to $125 at this level.

Pro offers a few key features over Plus, including the ability to generate six different builds concurrently, instead of one; 3D heatmap visualization; and the ability to purchase access to the Unity source code.

While higher annual gross revenue will push you into the more expensive tiers, smaller studios can still purchase Plus and Pro.

OTHER ENGINES

While Unity and Unreal are two of the most widely used engines, they aren't the only choices. **GameMaker Studio**[7] prices start at $39 per year per user for those that want to tinker. More expensive tiers allow you to publish on desktop and mobile platforms ($99 per year per user) and consoles ($399 per year per user).

[4] "Unity Personal," Unity.com. https://store.unity.com/products/unity-persona. (accessed January 25, 2018).
[5] "Unity Plus," Unity.com. https://store.unity.com/products/unity-plus. (accessed January 25, 2018).
[6] "Unity Pro," Unity.com. https://store.unity.com/products/unity-pro. (accessed January 25, 2018).
[7] "Product Choice," YoYoGames.com, https://www.yoyogames.com/get. (accessed February 23, 2018).

RPG Maker is tailored to (you guessed it!) RPGs. The most recent version, **RPG Maker MV, costs $79.99**[8]. The developers also offer **Visual Novel Maker for $59.99**[9].

MIDDLEWARE

In addition to your game engine, you might choose to use **middleware**[10] tools to streamline development. These typically have their own license fees, dictated by project budget size.

As you consider the resources you'll need to finish your game, make sure you account for costs related to middleware tools. These might not be overly cumbersome, but you don't want to get hit with a $1,000 expenditure you weren't counting on.

For instance, **Wwise**[11] (a widely used audio tool) is an affordable $750 per platform (PC, each different console, etc.) for projects capping out at $150,000. That fee jumps to $6,000 for the first platform and $3,000 for additional platforms between $150,001 and $1.5 million projects. Any game more expensive than that scales up rapidly to $18,000 for the first platform and $12,000 for each additional one.

You also need to consider that there may be additional middleware licenses for DLC. For example, Wwise offers DLC licenses at the same three budget tiers for $600, $2,000, and $5,000. These allow developers to release as much DLC during a 12-month period as they'd like. Cosmetic add-ons (skins, for instance), do not require a DLC license in this case.

Alternatively, Wwise can be licensed on a royalty basis for 1 percent of gross revenues. If you're just starting out, there's also a free option for projects under $150,000, and non-commercial projects do not require a license until they transition into products for sale. In other words, you can tinker without having to pay a dime until you're ready.

---

[8] "RPGMaker MV," RPGMakerweb.com.
      http://www.rpgmakerweb.com/products/programs/rpg-maker-mv.
      (accessed February 23, 2018).
[9] "VN Maker," VisualNovelMaker.com. http://visualnovelmaker.com/.
      (accessed February 23, 2018).
[10] **Middleware** - While this term can mean different things, in video game development, middleware is often thought of as software that can add functionality and features. It's often used to make development easier.
[11] "Wwise for Games," Audiokinetic.com. https://www.audiokinetic.com/pricing/for-games/.
      (accessed January 24, 2018).

Other popular middleware solutions include:

- Bink (Video)
- Speedtree (Vegetation modeling)
- Nvidia Gameworks (Visual and physics effects)
- Umbra (Visual optimization)
- Morpheme (Modeling for hair and clothing)
- Elias (Adaptive music)
- FMOD (Sound effects engine)
- Fabric (Extends Unity's sound capabilities)

SOURCE CONTROL

Code repositories are vital for source control, especially as your team begins to grow. The two commonly used solutions are Bitbucket by Atlassian and Github.

Github's **current pricing**[12] starts at $7 per user and scales upwards as you build a team and need more people involved. Students can access Github's personal account tier for free.

Bitbucket is free for teams of five or fewer. **Pricing**[13] scales up to $5 per user per month for the most feature-rich tier.

DROPBOX

Having a centralized place to store documents and assets is important. Dropbox is one of many solutions that can help with this and make it easier to receive and distribute assets.

Dropbox offers a free solution, but you may require more space. **Paid accounts**[14] begin at $12.50 per month per user for 2 TB of space. At the $20 per month per user level, you gain access to unlimited space, better administrative controls, and audit logs for event tracking.

---

[12] "Plans for all workflows," Github.com. https://github.com/pricing. (accessed January 24, 2018).
[13] "Free for small teams. Priced to scale," Bitbucket.org. https://bitbucket.org/product/pricing?tab=host-in-the-cloud. (accessed January 25, 2018).
[14] "You use Dropbox. Why doesn't your company?" Dropbox.com. https://www.dropbox.com/business/landing-t61fl?_tk=sem_b_goog&_camp=&_kw=dropbox%20pricing|e&_ad=182341515558|1t1|c&gclid=Cj0KCQiA-qDTBRD-ARIsAJ_10yLpBx9j9I_7162KEUXhXJdx_qJHftI0Tijbbe8CUCIA0NAPZpg7xm8aAgSbEALw_wcB. (accessed January 24, 2018).

SLACK AND DISCORD

You'll want a convenient way to manage communications with your team, especially when you're working remotely with contractors. Slack has become the market leader, offering multiple text channels, direct messaging, plugin integration (including social media, scheduling, task management, and more), and voice and video calling.

Smaller teams can likely get by with the free service. However, if you opt not to pay, Slack will only store your most recent 10,000 messages. You can hit that cap quickly as your team grows.

Voice and video calling are also limited to one-on-one affairs. With the first tier of **paid accounts**[15] ($8 per user per month), that grows to 15 users per call (complete with screen sharing) and unlimited message retention. This is important, as many Slack users share files on the platform.

For those who wish to build a community discussion platform, Discord is a good solution used by a number of developers. At first glance, there are many similarities between Slack and Discord (even from a visual perspective). However, Discord has been built and branded with video game end users in mind. Its key differentiator is group voice chat available to all users in a channel (if they so choose).

Discord is completely free, with no paid services available at this time. For those currently using Skype or Teamspeak for community and clan management, Discord is a streamlined option designed specifically for this purpose.

---

[15] "Slack for teams," Slack.com. https://slack.com/pricing. (accessed January 24, 2018).

IN THIS CHAPTER, WE LEARNED....

1. What kinds of tools you might want to use during development.
2. How to plan for engine costs.

CHAPTER
TEN

WHY DO I NEED ATTORNEYS AND ACCOUNTANTS?

Lawyers and accountants fall under "general and administrative," which is near the bottom of your budget. Their costs should be considered in every budget you create. Getting by without a lawyer for an entire project is nearly impossible. You're either paying up front or in the end, but a lawyer always exists in there somewhere.

You may be thinking of an accountant as the person who handles your books year-end, but depending on where you live, there may very well be need for advice on tax relief and other opportunities. They may also charge you to file that paperwork if you don't want to handle it yourself. If you aren't an accountant or an attorney, you're unlikely to get through an entire project and its aftermath without needing one or both of those.

There are some situations that obviously require an attorney. For instance, if you've been arrested for committing a crime, you might want professional representation to keep you out of the slammer.

In civil matters, it's less clear when you need an attorney and when you can make a judgment call. In many cases, you'll want a lawyer's assistance creating documents that can be easily modified (and, if necessary, reviewed by counsel for legal compliance).

WHAT SHOULD I EXPECT TO PAY FOR AN ATTORNEY?

Attorney fees can vary from firm to firm. As you might expect, independent practitioners will often charge on the lower end of the range. Large firms carry significant overhead (like office space) that often leads to higher fees.

Expect to pay $200 or more per hour for an attorney's time. This does not include direct, out-of-pocket expenses like photocopying, courier services, and filing fees.

Attorneys will also bill for staff members, like legal assistants and paralegals, that assist with research and preparation. It's important to ask your attorney for an estimate for each matter.

For instance, a contract review might only take an hour. However, if you spend a lot of time on the phone with your lawyer, multiple reviews are required, the attorney is required to draft new language, or you need representation in negotiations, you will see your anticipated expenses grow quickly.

Many attorneys will give you options and estimated costs. Make the most of your time with an attorney. Gather your questions in advance of a phone call, provide all relevant materials up front, and be clear about what you want from the attorney. Wasted work with an attorney can add up quickly.

WHAT SORTS OF THINGS SHOULD AN ATTORNEY HELP ME WITH?

Attorneys aren't just for suing people (it's actually one of their most expensive uses and generally to be avoided). You're going to want a lawyer to craft the documents you'll use in your business for years to come. The last thing you want is a fatal flaw in your employment contract or employee handbook that can leave you exposed to major legal trouble.

Here are a few things you'll want an attorney to assist with:

FORMALIZING YOUR BUSINESS STRUCTURE

It's important that you formalize your studio as its own business entity as soon as possible. Operating as a sole proprietor exposes you to potential legal and financial hardship. Incorporation (United States and Canada), forming a limited liability company (United States), or forming a limited company (United Kingdom) can insulate your personal assets and liability.

While you might be able to fill out and file the paperwork yourself, an attorney may still prove useful. It's important to understand what each of the business structures means for your company's operations.

Ask questions and make an informed decision. It's cumbersome to make a shift in business structure later.

EMPLOYMENT CONTRACTS

You can probably get away with an offer letter detailing salary and benefits (instead of a contract) in most cases. However, an employment contract better protects your studio.

Having a comprehensive document that explicitly details rights and responsibilities for both employer and employee gives you a solid foundation at the start of the relationship. Employment agreements can contain a number of important items, including:

- Start date
- Salary, pay schedule, and other related terms
- Job title
- Work hours
- Company holidays, vacation, and sick time
- Grievance policies
- Termination policies (for instances with and without cause), as well as any strictures that may apply following the employee's departure (including non-competition agreements). Note that non-competition assertions may not be enforceable (depending on locale and specific situation) and typically require some kind of consideration, like an employment offer or a raise (if the clause is added later).

CONTRACTOR AGREEMENTS

As with employment contracts, contractor agreements set out specific rights and responsibilities for both parties. Given that your contractor is likely working with a number of clients and juggling multiple projects, you'll want to make sure that you're clear about your needs.

A contractor agreement will likely include the following:

- Fee schedule
- Payment schedule
- Deadlines
- Specific deliverables
- Confidentiality requirements

PAY PEOPLE ON TIME

It shouldn't have to be said, but we're going to anyway. Pay people on time.

The video game industry is small, and the pool of professional talent who can make games is even smaller. If you don't pay people on time, you run the risk of alienating potential partners that you might want on your team.

Failure to pay people on time is often due to poor planning rather than malice. And that's why we focus on cash flow in both *The GameDev Business Handbook* and this book.

Make sure you're tracking when your contractors expect to be paid. Don't forget to pay your employees (a payroll service is a good idea). Being an employer means that people rely on you to eat and pay their rent. It's an important responsibility that should be taken seriously when building a business that will stand the test of time.

EMPLOYEE HANDBOOKS

Your employment contracts cover the foundational elements of your relationship. An employee handbook offers up more specifics about policies and procedures.

In many cases, these are important elements that wouldn't be appropriate for a contract. However, many employment contracts do require that employees read and acknowledge (by signature) that workers will adhere to those policies.

Employee handbooks typically include:

- Code of conduct and disciplinary procedures
- Expense authorization and reimbursement policy and procedure
- Whistleblower policy
- **Agency**[1] issues, including who may or may not speak to the media
- Social media policy
- Physical and digital security matters
- Substance abuse policy

These documents can updated as necessary. Depending on what you're changing, you might want to consult an attorney to ensure legal compliance and clarity.

IF MY ATTORNEY GETS ALL THIS DONE FOR ME, WHY DO I NEED AN ACCOUNTANT?

An attorney will help you navigate all the legal matters for your establishing and running your studio. Your accountant is going to be your go-to for ongoing financial management questions.

When you're starting up, you'll want to formalize your business structure. An attorney will help you understand the legal impact of the different choices (you can read more about this in Chapter 3 of *The GameDev Business Handbook*). An accountant will demystify tax and other financial implications.

---

[1] **Agency** - An implied or explicit agreement detailing how and when an employee may act on behalf of an employer. In some employment contracts, it's clear who is authorized to speak to the press.

Should you need to deal with royalties, your attorney will draft the agreement. Your accountant will help you set up the tools to track and report secondary payments and the metrics on which they are calculated.

In many regions, you'll be responsible for tracking, reporting, and paying income-based taxes (sales tax in the United States and VAT in the UK are two examples). It's important that you calculate this accurately and remit payments in a timely fashion. Your accountant will help you set up the systems required to stay on the right side of tax collectors.

IN THIS CHAPTER,
WE LEARNED....

1.   Why attorneys are important.
2.   How to plan for legal fees.
3.   When you'll want an accountant's help.

EPILOGUE

ADVICE FROM THE INDUSTRY

One of our favorite parts of interviewing for *The GameDev Business Handbook* was asking members of the industry to share their most valuable advice for developers just starting out. The guidance we were able to share inspired us to repeat the process for *The GameDev Budgeting Handbook*.

Without restriction or guidance on topic, each interviewee offered insightful perspectives from years in the video game industry. In the following pages, you'll find some additional tips about budgeting and more. In fact, much of the guidance is focused on creating the culture that the budgets support.

The varied responses are a final bit of advice before you dive into your budgeting spreadsheets. They are the reminders that a budget is a means to build a healthy business and achieve your creative vision.

RYAN BLACK
Lawyer and Partner, McMillan LLP

Love what you do.

First, love what you do and dedicate yourself to it—that sounds like a platitude, but enjoying the thing you do really helps make all the difficult work, stress, and tears worth it. When you bring passion to a project, it not only helps guide you through difficult times—and reward you for success!—but it helps you engage properly with advisors, colleagues, employees and consultants.

More substantively, make sure that you get some good professional advice at an early stage: the friend you know who went to law school might know someone you can chat with, or often it's not hard to find a lawyer in your area who would be willing to talk by phone for a brief time, even if just to point out some issues. Treat it like a legitimate, necessary business expense, because it is. Legal and accounting advice are both something you should at some point pay for, and hopefully as early as possible, because it is usually more cost effective to do things right the first time, rather than fixing a problem down the road. Many lawyers—at least in Canada—don't charge for that initial prospecting call. Be genuine about it—professional advisors are not in the business of giving away free advice, but if you're prepared to actually spend a little bit of money on professional advice, you can find the right person and make sure that you're getting good value for it. Ideally the advisors will be well-versed in video game topics, or otherwise familiar with helping startup, emerging or technology companies, in order to can guide you through the biggest issues, and away from the biggest mistakes, that companies often make. Getting good advice, whether as an employee, contractor, or business owner, is ultimately about protecting yourself and setting yourself up for longer term success.

ROBERT BROWN
Founder, Stride PR

Shop around for the best fit.

When it comes to selecting a PR agency, perform your due diligence. Talk with multiple agencies, inquire about their experience, team's experience, pricing and other games they've worked on to find the right agency for you.

ASHLY BURCH
Voice Actor (*Life is Strange, Horizon: Zero Dawn*)

Get some sleep!

Make a project because it speaks to you, not solely because you think it'll sell. Game development takes a long time and a lot of hard work, and if you don't love what you're making, you won't have the energy or drive to sustain yourself. Also, try to get some sleep, dangit!

SUDARSHAN RANGANATHAN
Head of Gaming, Ixie Games

Don't skimp on testing.

Always keep a budget for QA. Even if the QA is minimal, I always recommend to have a formal testing before showcasing the game to anyone. I have had a stint as a producer and every time a developer has approached me saying it's working now and the issue has been fixed, I did manage to find issues most of the times. Even when the code is well written and optimized, there are always chances when one can overlook a scenario where it will not work. Having QA performed formally on the game will make a whole world of difference between it being decent to fabulous.

NICK JOHNSON
Founder, Affect Accountancy

Accounting software can make your life easier.

A young developer who mainly works for corporate clients should consider registering for VAT even if their taxable income is less than the threshold—currently £85,000—so that they can reclaim VAT on software expense, office rent and professional services etc. It is fairly straightforward to report VAT and other taxes to HM Revenue & Customs, but you should take professional advice to make sure that you are set up property and using a good software package—I would recommend www.Xero.com which can automate the majority of your tax and accounting needs.

STEVEN MANSHIP
Lead Cinematics, Ninja Theory

Don't be afraid to ask for help.

Be confident. In yourself, in your talents, in your ideas, and in your projects. But also don't be afraid to admit when you don't know something, and be quick to hunt out the people that do know.

JAYSON NAPOLITANO
Label Manager, Scarlet Moon Productions

Stick with it.

The first is don't get discouraged. Game development is hard. Especially your first few times out, and with small teams, it's a lot to take on. But keep at it. Sometimes making something small out of the gate can fund the dream project you really want to make.

Also, you get what you pay for. If you want your talent to take care of you, you need to take care of them. That includes reasonable compensation, whether it be upfront money, revenue share, or rights. Let's all take care of each other and make awesome things together, because we're all in this because we love this medium!

DALE NORTH
Composer (*Pac-Man Pop, Ray's the Dead*)

Don't lose your passion for the medium.

I think everyone in the game process, whether it be us contractors and all the types of contractors, all the way up to people that are the head of these mega companies, outside of some rare anomalies, I think all of us value being a part of this so much that we hate being left out. We want to be a part of it as much as we can and if you can remember that no matter how busy you get or how big it gets, I think that helps make a game good more than a lot of these other considerations. It's that people make stuff for games, whether it be music or audio or UI or whatever, because they love video games.

2

1

It's really easy to forget that when we're all kind of just doing our own for-hire thing throughout the day. When developers work with us, they might know that in the beginning, but when it comes to the actual process of doing it, I feel like we forget that sometimes, that man, I put your game in and I'm happy that I worked on it, and then when level one one comes up and the first action and you see something happening set to your music, that's just like the best feeling ever. That's what everyone's going for is just that, "Oh, I was a part of something big and great," and I just hope that people remember that.

TOM OHLE
Founder, Evolve PR

Discoverability is challenging, so show off your game's unique features.

Make a great game with as many potential hooks as possible—anything that can be of interest to your target audience—and be prepared to work your ass off to get attention. There are so many games out there, and every developer is trying to reach the same media and influencers; those people get hundreds of email pitches every day from developers just like you, and even if you have a great game, they may not even see it due to the sheer quantity of content thrown in their faces. Everything cool that you can show off, whether it's through social media, in a trailer, at events, wherever, will be an opportunity to get attention. If you don't have anything cool to show, or you just don't take the time to show anyone, you're in for a tough ride.

ANDREW PARSONS
Producer, Devolver Digital

Make time for self-care.

Putting together a budget can be a challenge, for sure, but the best place to start is with all the known variables. Start with how much your cost of living is, whether you need hardware or software and then your basic staff costs. That should form the basis of your budget. What I like to see is someone that is dedicated enough to say "I want to spend my life doing this, and here's what that means in practical terms." If I see a low budget, I tend to think "well, are they getting their money from somewhere else, or are they moonlighting a job at Starbucks to make ends meet?" Because truly amazing games are rarely made as a part-time hobby. When it comes down to it, this is a business and you need to treat it as such. Other things which spring to mind are: Are you self-employed or do you want to start a company? Will tax or overheads be involved in that? Maybe there is some kind of state or grant-based funding which you can tap in to? Have you considered contingency in the case that you fall ill, or you want to go on honeymoon and will need a few weeks off?

None of these questions are designed to trip developers up or trick people—they are there to make sure that you're super realistic from the outset and that you know exactly what you're letting yourself in for.

I guess the final thing I'd say when it comes to budgeting is that you need to be mindful that the world doesn't end when you make a game. Build in some time for a break, time to show your game, time to have a breakdown if you need it. Because if you spend your time worrying about money, you're not worrying about the game. And if there's one thing you should be worried about above all else, it's the quality of your game.

STEPHANIE THOENSEN
PR & Events Manager, Psyonix

Be honest with yourself.

Be realistic about the game you are creating and the community you think it will touch. Working in games PR for over 10 years I have worked with many different companies and creators, and there's nothing worse than someone who is unrealistic about their own project and the amount of people or type of people that will be interested. I understand that every game is somebody's baby, but trying to do too much or getting mad at press and lashing out will only end in disaster.

WALT WILLIAMS
Writer (*Spec Ops: The Line, Star Wars Battlefront II*)

Learn from your failures.

Finish everything you start, even if it's not perfect. Every project teaches you something, even the failures. And it's better to have a portfolio full of flawed games than a collection of incomplete demos. This is the most marketable skill you'll ever have, and the surest path to success.

SHAMS JORJANI
Vice president of business development, Paradox

Plan for a career, not just a hit game.

Are you planning on retiring after making your first game? No, I didn't think so. Besides, your first game will probably be the worst game you ever make. Set yourself up so you get to make that tenth game, which will be great. This means work long term, don't be afraid to kill your darlings, sacrifice or even better, sell, your babies. Bring on people who allow you to focus on what you want to do. This includes a business person/CEO—who incidentally will be more inclined to join cheaply against equity compared to a dev resource.

RHIANNA PRATCHETT
Writer (*Tomb Raider, Rise of the Tomb Raider*)

Don't ruin relationships.

Wherever possible, avoid burning bridges. Burning bridges can feel very, very satisfying in the moment, but it generally—as a business practice—is not a good idea. And especially if you're up-and-coming in the industry, you don't want to start burning bridges right then. Just try and find ways through any difficulties, and try your best to be professional and diplomatic and polite. Try and treat everyone as you would wish to be treated really. Don't be a dick.

ELLA ROMANOS
Developer and industry consultant, Ella Romanos ltd.

Don't let a job title hold you back.

When you're starting out, your job title doesn't mean anything. What matters is responsibility and accountability. The reality is that you'll wear 10 different hats every day.

A job title is needed for external purposes. When starting up, what you actually need to ensure first and foremost is that you define who's responsible for what.

ZOI VITSENTZOU
Head of global operations, MoGi Group

Prepare for success long before launch.

My advice would be to think of the bigger picture. Think of the world outside of your game too. Always try to be as holistic as possible in shaping how your players experience your game, both in-game and out. Get the right community management team to get the buzz going online and across social media before the game launches, prep your player support branch before launch so they can be ready for incoming requests and communications as well as improving your player's experience and showing them that you care about them.

Having your localization done for all your key markets is important too. I'm not saying you need to translate into every language straight away, but it's important to determine key markets and have those localizations prepared for launch day.

TUUKKA TAIPALVESI
Executive Producer, Remedy Entertainment

Don't overpromise.

Smaller indies are tempted to please publishers, because you want to get into the market. You want to work on your passion, so you might end up promising 150 percent of what your time and budget actually allows. You're setting up yourself for crunch from the get-go.

You will be in an unsustainable situation. Be careful what you plan for and be careful what you sell to the publisher, because the publisher will hold you to it. You have no bargaining power as a small indie. You need to be careful with your initial planning and budgeting so that you consider the unforeseen.

Don't make life too hard for yourself just because you love what you're doing. It's easy to promise way too much, more than you can deliver. The problem for new developers is they don't often know how much they can deliver. They see the fast progress that the game makes in the very early phases of pre-production and they get excited, 'This is going super well! Everything's on schedule!'

Then you hit production and you have to do the same thing over and over and over, and it's not fun anymore. It's work and that is something that a new developer needs to take into account.

This is still a job. It's not a hobby, and you need to have work-life balance. You need to plan according to what you can do, what your family situation is, what your financial situation is and what you want out of the end product.

NIKO STARK
Financial Controller, Remedy Entertainment

Learn the ropes at a company that shares your values.

Start in a company with steady business. You can have dreams of a startup, but it won't be easy. So get familiar with the industry, and go out there and talk with people. The atmosphere in this industry is great. You can talk with anyone and get answers and advice.

You'll see both mistakes and opportunities. You'll know what works and what doesn't.

AUSTIN WINTORY
BAFTA Award winning and Grammy Award nominated composer (*Journey, Assassin's Creed Syndicate*)

It's OK to rock the boat.

The advice I generally can't resist offering people, regardless of if it's a composer or a developer or a writer, or whatever, is to embrace being divisive. The reason I say that is because when we haven't gotten our feet on the ground professionally, there's a survival instinct that kicks in and an overwhelming need to be approved and loved by both the general public and our colleagues.

Our instinct is to be approved and not rock the boat. We fight these competing interests to be ourselves and to also be part of the collective. I see it especially with composers, because there are some very strong trends that are loaded with cliches, and so I see composers who just dive straight in and start writing music that's completely indistinguishable from the endless piles out there. Don't do that.

I recognize it's a lot easier to say than to do, but still, fight that urge, because the less you do that, the more you become you. Ultimately, that's far more valuable. So don't be afraid to turn people away, because you have just as much a chance of turning someone toward you in the process.

Embrace whatever it is that you love. If you're the king of AAA, and all you want to do is score Call of Duty games and Rockstar games, then fine. But if your thing is to be the person responsible for the next *Gone Home*, then great. Own that.

And if the person that you're meeting with doesn't respond to that, you do both of you a favor by making who you are plain, because it's not going to work out down the road as a collaboration if it turns out you're wildly in different places philosophically, musically, and professionally. The sooner that's known, the sooner you bond or realize it isn't a great fit.

APPENDIX – USING THE BUDGET TEMPLATES

Now that you've spent some time learning how we put our sample budgets together, it's time to take the plunge yourself. With your data and the formulas built into the templates, you'll start to get a complete picture of your game development costs quickly.

We recommend you make digital copies of the templates, ensuring you always have a blank one to start from. This can be done by duplicating the sheets in the same workbook, or copying the sheet to another workbook. Yes, you have our permission to make copies for personal use, but you may not redistribute the samples and templates.

Some other things you should know:

- The three templates each include clearly marked cells where you should enter information. Only fill in the bright yellow cells to ensure you don't overwrite those important formulas.
- There are notes in many of the cells. For more information, simply hover over the cell to bring up the accompanying text.
- You can add or subtract rows and columns or change the timing on the different project phases to customize the templates. However, this will alter formulas.
    - If you add columns or change the timing of project phases, you will need to amend the formulas underneath the cash flow tracker at the bottom. These are highlighted in magenta. These cells are simple sums that add the expenses for all of the months in a specific phase.
    - If you add staff or contractors, you need to ensure that the formulas that handle department subtotals are updated. Those cells are highlighted in green. The subtotal cells are calculated by adding all of the position costs for the month (hours multiplied by the hourly rate in column D). Follow the

formula format to add new positions to the calculation.
- Formulas that simply sum rows, columns, or cell ranges should dynamically change upon the addition of new rows and columns.
- As explained in Chapter 1, we calculate out 174 dev-hours per month. This closely models a 52-week year.

The "First project without funding" template functions differently than the other two. First, there is a distinction between founder salaries (which will likely be foregone or reimbursed later) and expenses related to contracted workers that must be paid in a timely fashion. Additionally, the cash flow tracker at the bottom requires out of pocket contributions to cover monthly expenses, as there are no disbursements from an outside funding source.

When you start working with the other two templates, customization becomes even more important. While you'll have an idea of when you'd like your milestones set and how much money you want assigned to each, those details will ultimately be negotiated by you and your funder/publisher.

As you are negotiating, plug numbers into your budget and see how they impact your ability to maintain positive cash flow. Remember, once you dip into the red, someone isn't getting paid. Failing to meet your financial obligations can start you on a disastrous path, causing work stoppages, project delays, and negative impact on your reputation (and ultimately your ability to attract employee and contractor candidates).

We urge you to spend time playing with the budget templates to get a feel for how the formulas work. Play around with adding, subtracting, and moving rows and columns. Becoming familiar with the tools early can prepare you to make smarter, faster decisions about your financial position later, when it counts. **Just remember to make copies of the templates, so you can always start over with an untarnished blank in case you accidentally break the formulas and can't figure out how to repair them.**

INDEX

A

AAA *26, 105, 117, 133, 135, 144*
Abrams Artists *114*
Abzu *84*
accountant *16–17, 18, 37–38, 52, 56, 151–157, 163*
adoption *127*
Affect Group *52, 56, 163*
agency *155*
Amazon *85*
American Society of Composers, Authors, and Publishers (ASCAP) *96, 97*
Arno, Christian *72*
Assassin's Creed *85*
Assassin's Creed Syndicate *81, 91, 171*
asset creation *104*
Atlas *114*
Atlassian *147*
attorney. *See* lawyer
at will employment *46*
audience engagement *138*

B

back end. *See* royalties
BAFTA *81, 117*
Bandcamp *85, 85–86*
barks *104*
Bink *147*
Bitbucket *147*
Black, Ryan *47–49, 48–49, 161*
boilerplate *65*
bottom-line *24*
Brexit *59*
Broadcast Music, Inc. (BMI) *96*
Brown, Robert *130–131, 132–133, 133, 134, 162*

bug reports *68*
Burch, Ashly *114, 115, 118–120, 162*
burn rate *28*
business development *27, 28–29, 29–30, 30–32, 33, 35–36, 169–170*
business structure *153*

C

Canada Pension Plan *49*
Canada Revenue Agency *47, 48, 50*
cash flow *12, 18, 20, 64*
Cast Away *81*
CESD *114*
cinematics *104, 117*
Clash of Clans *30*
Clash Royale *30*
Clueless Gamer *137*
code of conduct *155*
community development *128, 140, 169*
comping *83*
composer *15–16, 75–99, 164–166*
composition *95, 96*
console test units *68*
contract *152, 153, 155*
contractor *41–61, 154*
contractors *16, 17, 24, 27, 31, 34*
contracts *92–93*
copyist *83*
credit *110*
CRI *79*
crisis planning *129*
critical path *102*
Crowley, Dale *79*
Crusader Kings *30*
cue *88*

D

Dance Central *95*
Dead Island *136*
delay *13, 36–37*
dependent contractor *47, 48*
Designing Music Now *84–85*
desk-side demos *129*
dev-hours *13, 25–26*
dev-months *13, 20, 23–38*
Devolver Digital *28–29, 35–36,*
166–167
digital recordist *83*
director. *See* officer
disability insurance *45, 50*
disclosure *138*
Discord *148*
discoverability *38, 127–128, 166*
DmC: Devil May Cry *118,*
123–124
DPN *114*
Dropbox *147*
DropMix *95*

E

Electronics Entertainment Expo
(E3) *17, 128, 129, 139*
Elias *79, 147*
employee *41–61*
employee assistance program
50
employee contract. *See* contract
employee handbook *152*
employee handbooks *155*
employment insurance *49*
employment law (Canada)
46–50
employment law (UK) *52–57*
employment law (United States)
42–45
End User License Agreement
(EULA) *144*
Enter the Gungeon *28*
Epic Games *144–145*

equity *15*
esports *140*
Europa Universalis *30*
European Economic Area *59*
event demos *129*
Evolve PR *128–129, 130,*
131–132, 133–135, 137, 138–
139, 166
exclusivity *110*
expense policy *155*
extended health care *50*

F

Fabric *79, 147*
family leave *50*
Federal Insurance Contribution
Act (FICA) *44*
field recording *94*
first-party relations *66*
FMOD *79, 147*
French, Italian, German, and
Spanish (FIGS) *69–72, 72*

G

Game Developers Conference
(GDC) *17, 102, 129*
game engine *144–146*
GameMaker Studio *145*
Games as a Service *139–141,*
140
game trailer *136–137*
Gehbauer, Cheryl *95–98*
Gelatt, Phillip *104*
Giant Squid *84*
Giant Studios *123*
Github *147*
Goldberg, Daniel *31–32*
grievance *153*
Gusto *44*

H

Hanks, Tom *81*
Harmonix *95–98*
health insurance *42, 45*
Hellblade: Senua's Sacrifice *117,*
118, *123–124*
Henley, Hilary *59*
Her Majesty's Revenue &
Customs (HMRC) *52, 56, 57,*
163
Hicks, Kole *84–85, 94*
holiday pay. *See* vacation
Hollywood *104*
Horizon: Zero Dawn *114, 162*
Hotline Miami *28*

I

incidental dialog *116*
incorporation *153*
indie darling *135*
intellectual property *80*
Internal Revenue Service (IRS)
42
iTunes *85, 86*
Ixie Gaming *67–69, 162*

J

Jeong, Sarah *95*
job title *153, 169*
Johnson, Nick *52, 56, 163*
Jorjani, Shams *30–32, 33, 34,*
168
Journey *81, 84, 171*
Juergens, Melina *117*
jurisdiction *49*

K

key performance indicators (KPI)
138–139
Kickstarter *85*
kill points *111*

L

lawyer *16–17, 38, 47–49, 51, 59,*
75, 151–157, 161
leaves of absence *46*
legal assistant *152*
librarian *83*
licensing *16, 76, 86–87, 95–98,*
144, 146
life insurance *45*
Life is Strange *114, 162*
limited company *153*
limited liability company *153*
Lingo24 *72*
live game. *See* Games as a
Service
localization *38, 66, 69–72, 169*
localization quality assurance
(LQA) *72*
lyrics *95*

M

Manship, Steve *117, 118,*
120–122, 122–124, 164
marketing *38, 65*
master (music) *95, 96*
maternity *53*
McMillan *47–49, 48–49, 50, 51,*
59, 161
media *128, 137*
media training *129, 129–130*
Medicare *44*
Metacritic *139*
middleware *79, 146–147*
milestone *18, 30, 64, 65, 109*
minimum wage *46, 53*
misclassification (employement)
57
MoGi Group *70–71, 169*
Morpheme *147*
motion capture. *See* performance
capture

music *15–16, 75–99, 164*

N

Napolitano, Jayson *78, 80, 89, 164*
narrative designer *101–112*
national insurance *56*
Ninja Theory *117, 118, 120–122, 123–124, 164*
non-competition agreement *153*
non-disclosure agreement *116*
North American Free Trade Agreement (NAFTA) *58*
North, Dale *76–78, 78, 88, 90, 164*
notice period *53*
Nvidia Gameworks *147*

O

O'Brien, Conan *137*
offer letter *153*
officer *55*
Ohle, Tom *128–129, 130, 131–132, 133–134, 137, 138–139, 166*
OpenCritic *139*
orchestra *83*
overage *23*
overhead *34, 152*
Overlord *105*
Overlord II *105*
overtime *46*

P

package deal *82–85*
Pac-Man Pop *76*
paid time off *42*
Paradox Interactive *30–32, 33, 34, 168*
paralegal *152*
Parsons, Andrew *28–29, 35–36,*

166–167
paternity *53*
PAX *17, 128, 129, 139*
payment terms *80*
payroll service *154*
pension *56, 109*
per diem *65*
performance capture *113–125*
performance royalty organization (PRO) *95, 96*
performer (music) *96*
personal days *45, 50*
personal service company *56*
PR *162*
Pratchett, Rhianna *103, 104–105, 106–107, 109, 110, 168*
press relations. *See* public relations (PR)
producer (music) *95–96, 96*
professional development *45*
Psyonix *139–141, 167*
public relations agency *130–132*
public relations (PR) *65, 111, 127–141, 161, 166, 167*
publisher *18, 27–29, 63–73, 135, 136–137, 144, 144–145, 166–167, 169–170*
publisher (music) *96*

Q

quality assurance (QA) *37, 66, 67–69, 162*

R

Ranganathan, Sudarshan *67–69, 162*
Ranger, Michel *51*
Ray's the Dead *76*
recording studio *82, 83, 84–85, 120–122*
record label *96*

recoup *64, 65–66*
Reid, Mike *50*
Remedy Entertainment *27, 29–30, 169–170*
Resident Evil *113*
retirement savings *45*
revenue share. *See* royalties
revisions (writing) *108–109*
Rise of the Tomb Raider *103, 104, 105, 168*
risk *30*
Rock Band *95*
Rocket League *139–141*
Romanos, Ella *24, 32, 34, 169*
royalties *16, 17, 87, 115, 144, 145, 156*
RPG Maker *146*

S

Sagaz Test *47–48*
salary *153*
SBV *114*
Scarlet Moon Productions *78, 81, 92–93, 164*
Screen Actors Guild - American Federation of Television and Radio Artists (SAG-AFTRA) *110, 114, 115*
self-care *166–167*
sentiment *138*
share of voice *138*
sick leave *42, 45, 50, 53, 153*
sides *114, 119*
signatory *115*
Silvestri, Alan *81*
Skype *148*
Slack *148*
social media *129, 130, 137, 138, 155, 166, 169*
software as a service (SaaS) *16*
sole proprietor *153*
Somatone Interactive *79*

songwriter *96*
sound design *94*
soundtrack *76, 81, 85–86*
source control *147*
Spec Ops: The Line *102, 168*
Speedtree *147*
Stafford, John *105*
stakeholder *103*
Stark, Niko *27, 170*
Star Wars Battlefront II *102, 168*
statutory Holidays *46*
Steam *85, 127, 128*
Stoic Studio *87*
storefronts *66*
Stride PR *130–131, 132–133, 133, 134, 162*
strike *115*
studio engineer *83, 85*
substance abuse *155*
Sumthing Else Music *86*
Supercell *30*
Surviving Mars *30*
systemic content *102*

T

T-65b Records *86*
Taipalvesi, Tuukka *29–30, 169–170*
talent agent *114*
tax credits *51*
taxes *42, 50, 151, 155*
Teamspeak *148*
termination *46, 53, 153*
The Banner Saga *87*
The International Game Developers Association (IGDA) *102*
The Verge *95*
The Witcher *105*
The Wizard of Oz *75*
Thoensen, Stephanie *139–141, 167*

Tomb Raider *103*, *105*, *168*
top-level budget *27*
trailer *166*
transparency *138*
travel *65*
Triple-A. *See* AAA
triple-I *80*
Triumph Studios *105*
Twitch *137*
Twitter *130*

U

UBILOUD *86*
Ubisoft *85–86*, *105*
Umbra *147*
unemployment insurance *42, 44*
union *110, 114, 115–116*
Unity *145*
Unreal Engine *144–145*
user experience *67*
user testing. *See* quality assurance
(QA)

V

vacation *45, 46, 50, 53, 153,
166–167*
value-added tax (VAT) *156, 163*
Vicon *124*
Vitsentzou, Zoi *70–71, 169*
voice acting *113–125, 162*
voice director *118*
voiceover *66*
volume *122*

W

whistleblower policy *155*
Williams, Walt *102–103, 103,
106, 108, 109, 168*
Wintory, Austin *81–82, 84, 86,
87, 88–89, 90–94, 171*
worker (employment class) *52*

worker's compensation *50*
work hour restrictions *46*
work hours *153*
work visa *58–60*
writer *101–112, 168*
Writers Guild of America (WGA)
109, 110
Writers' Guild of Great Britain,
The *109, 110*
Wwise *79, 146*

X

Xero *163*

Y

YouTube *113, 137*

Z

Zemeckis, Robert *81*

ABOUT THE AUTHOR

After leaving behind a career in nonprofit funding, Michael Futter put his MBA to work as a journalist covering business and legal issues. During that time, he wrote countless stories about independent developer successes (many of whom are featured in his books, *The GameDev Business Handbook* and *The GameDev Budgeting Handbook*). Michael lives in New Jersey with his family.

Made in the USA
Middletown, DE
13 January 2019